*My [...] [...] with [...] friendship.
Radha.*

# Mediating Migration

**Global Media and Communication**

Adrian Athique, *Indian Media*
Jean K. Chalaby, *The Format Age*
Terry Flew, *Global Creative Industries*
Myria Georgiou, *Media and the City*
Radha Sarma Hegde, *Mediating Migration*
Noha Mellor, Khalil Rinnawi, Nabil Dajani and Muhammad I.
  Ayish, *Arab Media*
Shani Orgad, *Media Representation and the Global Imagination*
Stylianos Papathanassopoulos and Ralph Negrine, *European Media*

# Mediating Migration

RADHA SARMA HEGDE

polity

First published in 2016 by Polity Press

Polity Press
65 Bridge Street
Cambridge CB2 1UR, UK

Polity Press
350 Main Street
Malden, MA 02148, USA

ISBN-13: 978-0-7456-4632-9
ISBN-13: 978-0-7456-4633-6 (pb)

A catalogue record for this book is available from the British Library.

Library of Congress Cataloging-in-Publication Data

Names: Hegde, Radha Sarma, 1953-
Title: Mediating migration / Radha S. Hegde. Description: Cambridge, UK ; Malden, MA : Polity, [2015] | Series: Global media and communication | Includes bibliographical references and index. Identifiers: LCCN 2015022617| ISBN 9780745646329 (hardcover : alk. paper) | ISBN 0745646328 (hardcover : alk. paper) | ISBN 9780745646336 (pbk. : alk. paper) | ISBN 0745646336 (pbk. : alk. paper) Subjects: LCSH: Mass media and immigrants. | Mass media and social
   integration. | Mass media and culture. | Immigrants--Social networks. |
   Immigrants--Cultural assimilation. | Emigration and immigration--Social
   aspects. | Emigration and immigration--Technological innovations.
Classification: LCC P94.5.I48 H44 2015 | DDC 302.23086/91--dc23 LC record available at http://lccn.loc.gov/2015022617

Typeset in 11 on 13pt Adobe Garamond Pro by
Servis Filmsetting Ltd, Stockport, Cheshire
Printed and bound in the UK by CPI Group (UK) Ltd, Croydon, CR0 4YY

For further information on Polity, visit our website: politybooks.com

To Krishna, who has journeyed with me.

# Contents

# Acknowledgments

This book has emerged from my long-standing scholarly interest in the politics and narratives of migration. Writing the book has itself been a journey of sorts, on which I have been sustained and supported by many. The chapters all grew and developed from conversations with colleagues and friends, lectures in classes, discussions with students, and presentations delivered at various academic institutions.

For some years now, I have been teaching on the subjects of migration, media, and globalization. These courses have served as a testing ground for many of the ideas presented in this book. I wish to acknowledge my graduate and undergraduate students at New York University who have been intellectually curious, responsive, and involved with my work.

Each of the chapters was shaped over the course of an academic and social journey. I am deeply appreciative of the scholars who have engaged and invited me to present my work when it was still evolving and in formation. These interactions have been crucial to the completion of this book. Many of the ideas in the introduction were shaped in two keynote addresses that I delivered, the first at a conference arranged by the Academy of Finland, and the next at the Nordic Network for Media and Migration, University of Helsinki. My thanks to Karina Horsti, Minna Aslama, and Petteri Pietikäinen. The ideas for chapter 2 were inspired by my meetings with young undocumented activists in New York City. I presented the arguments of this chapter in a panel at the International Communication Association conference along with Karina Horsti, Mirca Madianou, Tanja Thomas, and Elke Grittmann, to all of whom I extend my thanks. Parts of chapter 3 were presented at St. Louis University at Madrid and also at the University of Western Washington. My thanks to Brian Goss, Rae Lynn Schwartz-DuPre, Angharad Valdivia, Cameron McCarthy, and Natalie Fenton for their engagement with the ideas and arguments presented in that chapter. Parts of chapter 4 have also been presented at Freie Universität Berlin, where I deeply value the collegiality of Margreth Lünenborg and Elfriede Fürsich. Chapter 5 took shape in presentations at the University of Wisconsin, Madison, at the Crossroads in Cultural Studies Conference in Paris, and at the Diasporic Foodways Conference at the University of Toronto. My thanks to Ajaya Sahoo and the referees for valuable editorial input on a version of this chapter that was published in the *Journal of South Asian Diaspora*. Chapter 6 on music, technology, and the diaspora has benefited greatly from discussions that followed presentations at Cambridge University, Yale University, the University of California, Riverside, and the University of Hyderabad. For these opportunities and conversations, I wish to thank Mirca Madianou, Inderpal Grewal, Susan Ossman, Usha Raman, Vinod Pavarala, Aparna Rayaprol, and Amit Kumar Mishra. My thanks to Cynthia Carter and Lisa McLaughlin of *Feminist Media Studies* for their constant support. A very special thanks to Shani Orgad and Linda Steiner for their input, timely comments, and extremely helpful suggestions. To Linda, a special thanks for instant advice on sentences that go astray. I am also grateful to the activists, food bloggers, and musicians who generously gave me of their time and whose narratives I have incorporated into the book.

The intellectual space, support, and stimulation I have received at New York University, and especially from my colleagues in the Department of Media, Culture, and Communication, have been invaluable. For his rich intellectual mentorship and support, I owe my deep gratitude to Arjun Appadurai, my colleague, whose scholarship has been truly inspirational to my intellectual pursuits, and in particular to this book on migration. Arjun, thank you very much for all the stimulating conversations and for being most generous with your time. To Arvind Rajagopal, my deeply felt thanks for his sustained intellectual support, insightful conversations, and friendship. Over the years, I have learnt much from my friend and colleague Allen Feldman, and I am deeply grateful for the conversations we have had on many of the ideas presented here. To my colleagues Helen Nissenbaum and Deborah Borisoff, I would like to express my profound gratitude for their friendship and unswerving support of this project right from the very beginning. Checking in with Helen about (impossible) writing goals and logging our daily word counts has been crucial to the completion of this book. Debbie, thank you for your timely and dependable academic mentoring and keeping me centered with humor and friendship. To Marita Sturken and Lisa Gitelman – thank you for your collegiality and enabling various academic processes that helped me along the way.

There are several others who have helped shape this book through its growth and development. To Robert Wosnitzer, I wish to express my deep thanks for the many conversations and engaged discussions we have had along the way. Jacqueline Rohel and Laura Norén – thank you for your help and thoughtful suggestions, especially on the topic of food and food blogs. To my students, Uma Anand, Anya Kandel, Rahma Mian, Jonathan Zalman, Miriam Halsey, and Chris Nolan – thanks for the conversations, research help, and/or collectively alerting me to just about everything that was being written about migration anywhere in the world. Daniel Bloch has shared with me his avid interest in diasporic literature and film, introducing me to new publications, film events, and book releases. Danny, thanks for having been an important part of this journey from its very nascent stages.

Emily Goldsher-Diamond and Madhurim Gupta have worked tirelessly with me through the various aspects of getting this manuscript ready for publication. I simply could not have done it without them. Emily – I deeply appreciate the meticulous research assistance. Overcoming all time-space constraints, Madhurim has worked with me down to the wire on the final details. Madhurim – thank you very much. Andrea Drugan and Joe Devanny were both truly supportive of this endeavor and their encouragement was crucial to the launching of this project. Elen Griffiths of Polity Press has been simply wonderful to work with. Elen, thank you very much for your support, patience, and professionalism.

To Rita Chaudhuri I owe a special debt of gratitude for her steadfast friendship over the years. Thanks, Rita, for both steering and cheering me to the finish line.

Nirupama Shree, my daughter, has been ever ready to edit at short notice, and provide instant, honest critique. Thanks Niru, as always. Krishna – thank you for everything, too numerous to be named:

Radha Sarma Hegde
New York City; Chennai

A version of chapter 4 was published as Hegde, R. (2010) Eyeing Publics: Veiling and the Performance of Civic Visibility. In Brouwer, D. C. and Asen, R. (eds.) *Public Modalities*. University of Alabama Press, Tuscaloosa, AL, pp. 154–72. A version of chapter 5 was published as Hegde, R. (2014) Food Blogs and the Digital Reimagination of South Asian Diasporic Publics. *South Asian Diaspora* 6(1), 89–103.

# 1    Introduction

In the summer of 2008, an unverified piece of gossip made its way into the *Brazilian Voice*, an ethnic newspaper published in Newark, New Jersey. A report in the newspaper claimed that the winning ticket of the New Jersey state mega-millions lottery had been purchased by a Brazilian immigrant, at a supermarket in a neighborhood with a large Brazilian and Portuguese population. A guessing game began and conjectures started to fly. Was the winner an undocumented immigrant and therefore reluctant to claim the prize for fear of being deported? Another rumor claimed that the winner was from Governador Valadares, known as Brazil's most American city, and home to a large number of immigrants in the United States. While this news was bouncing back and forth between the United States and Brazil, the owner of the supermarket in Newark where the ticket was sold identified the winners and described them as humble, hardworking, and living the American dream.[1]

The plot line of this riveting story features the key themes of our times – immigration, communication, and speculation. Its global contours are shaped not only by the rapid travel of information through talk, text, Internet, telephone, and print, but also by the crisscrossing of intricate, transnational networks of connection. An ethnic newspaper that typically raises no fanfare rapidly converges with other forms of technology speeding up the global dispersal of information, revealing the continuing connections maintained between nations, homelands, and the diaspora. The rumor that ricocheted from Newark to Rio de Janeiro captures a basic premise of globalization: that an immigrant community's local identity is always already transnationally situated. The story itself, a public recital of the precarity of immigrant life, hinged on a familiar binary: was the winner legal or illegal? In the ethnic neighborhoods of Newark, the story raised a compelling question: what would an undocumented immigrant do in such a circumstance? After all, claiming the prize meant inviting the risk of being investigated. First and foremost, what was being evoked was the line separating the settled, legal migrant possessing papers from the undocumented migrant whose presence was unregistered and hence invisible. Migration has always been about navigating new risks, uncertainty, and the contested terrain of mobility. However, under the social conditions defined by the global economy and communication technologies, the politics and problematics of migration have been radically recalibrated.

Migration, a contested topic on national agendas, is at the forefront of current discourses on globalization. Political crises, instabilities, and deep structural inequities within countries and between nations have led to the increased flow of migrants in search of better economic opportunities and stable political conditions. Media representations of migrants frequently stir up controversies about the presence of the Other in the national imaginary. The public, particularly in the West, are routinely exposed to images of men, women, and children undertaking the harsh journey across Central America, migrants from North and Sub-Saharan Africa on their perilous sea voyages to reach Spain or Italy, or refugees fleeing war-torn regions like Syria, Afghanistan, or Iraq. These accounts are often sensationalized or exaggerated through the use of apocalyptic representations of exodus (de Haas, 2008), sometimes through the narrative of unassimilability and difference (Chavez, K. R., 2013), or through the entangled framing of migrants either as threat or as victims eligible for compassion (Horsti, 2003, 2013). We are witnessing both a surge in the number of irregular or undocumented migrants crossing borders and a significant increase in the efforts by governments worldwide to regulate and control the flow of migrants (Castles, de Haas, and Miller, 2013). Migratory flows have also intensified nationalist discourses and stirred up debates on border control, racial difference, immigration regulations, and the meaning of citizenship. As the growing structural demand for labor drives immigration and shapes the dreams of hopeful migrants particularly from the Global South, the repercussions are felt not only in terms of policy and state action, but also in the transformations of localities, markets, and lived experiences. In the contemporary context, the way in which these social and cultural changes are experienced is intricately connected to the world of media and communication.

The media, argue Mitchell and Hansen (2010: xxii), broker the giving of space and time within which concrete experience becomes possible, and "rather than determining our situation, we might better say media are our situation." The media frame the very manner in which the contemporary realities of migration are articulated and publicized. Hence media forms, communicative practices, and the nature of mediated connections have to be factored into current theorizations about migration. Issues about immigration and borders explode in transnational space even as they are sensationalized in new echo chambers of convergent media. It is through diverse and changing media practices that migrants themselves create networks of transnational connections and reimagine the meaning and reach of communities. Writing about globalization, Jameson (1999) notes that although it is by no means a new phenomenon, its definitional contours have changed due to the technological character of contemporary life. Similarly, media and communication technologies have redefined the terms and conditions of the migrant experience with reference to both the immediacy of connection and the urgency of its implications.

Media practices have historically shaped the imagining of forgotten pasts and possible futures. Old letters in shoeboxes, fading black-and-white images of distant histories, and long-distance telephone calls with crackly connections have given way to new media platforms and affordances, which now constitute the transformed epistolary base and the communication infrastructure of the migrant experience.[2] Electronic mediation and mass migration, according to Appadurai (1996: 4), "mark the world of the present not as technically new forces but as ones that seem to impel (and sometimes compel) the work of the imagination." This book builds on and extends a similar premise: that examining migration and mediation together provides a vantage point from which to understand the politics of mobility in the global present. There is a descriptive and not deterministic narrative to relate about the devices and technologies of reproduction that migrants now use to stay connected, to plan their pathways, manage their affective worlds, and navigate their contested locations. The discussions in this book follow Mitchell and Hansen's (2010: xv) suggestion: to take note of the shift in emphasis from media as artifactuality to media as processes of mediation. For instance, the point is not merely to view migrants as producers or consumers of one particular media form or another, but rather to understand how the cultural politics, social dynamics, and lived geographies of migrants are entrenched within media worlds. A less media-centric approach, as Morley (2011: 744) argues, which takes into account cross-border mobilities, "effectively places questions of media and communication in the broader frame of their material context and settings." Taking its cue from these lines of argument, this book contextualizes the complex constitutive connection between media forms and practices, mediated environments, and the politics of migration. Using diasporic itinerancy as a point of departure also forces a rethinking of assumptions that structure bounded and fixed understandings of community, belonging, communication, and location. In the chapters that follow, I offer a particular narration of migrant experiences as shaped by technologies of communication and the social, political, and economic configurations of globalization.

## Transnational Topographies of Affiliation

The arguments and descriptions in this book cohere around the perspective that the subject of immigration and the debates around it have to be understood in terms of their transnational and cross-border implications. Here in this section, I capture some aspects of these transnational entanglements that we need to consider in our contextualization of migration. Every story and crisis around immigration reveals that the subject of migration is neither linear nor contained within the nation-state. The dramatis personae involved, the issues and implications, are all geographically dispersed and yet transnationally interconnected. However, historically the study of migration has been framed by the centrality of the nation and the compartmentalization of immigration as an isolable subject that can be turned on and off according to national interests (Castles, 2002: 1145). Migrants and their relocated lives have for long been studied as modular, exchangeable units that move across borders. Writing about the state of research on Mexican migration to the United States, Rouse (1992: 47) notes that there has been a general tendency to oversimplify immigrant worlds, by construing them in "the anodyne language of adaptation, coping and fit." He argues that migration in general has been analyzed mainly in bipolar terms, where communities are conceptualized as autonomous bodies who simply shift their social ties from one community to another. These forms of reductive oversimplifications have been fairly common in the dominant approaches to the study of immigrants and borders in the social sciences. A strictly behavioral emphasis on studying the adaptation patterns of individuals and groups largely obscures the innovative practices and multi-layered relations that migrants forge as they construct new forms of transnational communities (see Glick-Schiller, Basch, and Szanton-Blanc, 1995).

The longevity of the nation and the individual, as organizing units of analysis in the research and policy on migration, has also limited our ability to examine the assemblage of factors within which the subject of migration is embedded (Sassen, 1998). While the nation-state remains the arbiter of immigration policy, the materiality of the migratory experience is deeply rooted in processes that cut across and between nations and cultures. The human drama of immigration and the everyday realities of mobile populations stand often in strong contrast to the official narratives of citizenship proclaimed by nations. As Quayson and Daswani (2013: 2) note, "taken together the concepts of diaspora and transnationalism promise a broad understanding of all the forms and implications that derive from the vast movements of populations, ideas, technologies, images, and financial networks that have come to shape the world we live in today." The multi-layered contexts and contested experiences of migration today require a critical rethinking of the ways in which the nation as a category is mobilized in the global present: a rethinking that critically works the idea of the trans-national in order to draw attention to the transformatory aspects of social life and imagination in the global present.[3]

In his eloquent, pioneering, and widely cited publication *Modernity at Large*, Appadurai theorizes the global disjunctures that exist between the econ-omy, culture, and politics through a series of interconnected landscapes (eth-noscapes, mediascapes, technoscapes, finanscapes, ideoscapes). He describes the "scapes" as "perspectival constructs inflected by the historical, linguistic and political situatedness of different sorts of actors" (Appadurai, 1996: 33). Appadurai's discussion of the various "scapes" has been profoundly important in shaping scholarly engagement with the fluid cultural forms of globaliza-tion, and the deterritorialized modalities of action and performance that drive transnational communities. Returning to the issues of global circulation, capital, infrastructure, and social justice, Appadurai (2006: 30) describes how the grounded, centralized, vertebrate structures of the nation are now encoun-tering the mobile, modular, and cellular forms of global capital:

> Returning to the always fragile idea of a world of national economies, we can characterize the current era of globalization – driven by the triple engines of speculative capital, new financial instruments, and high-speed information technologies – as creating new tensions between the wanton urge of global capital to roam without license or limit and the still regnant fantasy that the nation-state assures a sovereign economic space.

This distinction, yet dependence, between vertebrate and cellular systems captures the crisis of circulation and the nature of capitalism in the contem-porary context.[4] Appadurai's provocative model and insightful arguments open up lines of inquiry about the transformations in the interdependent fields of migration and global capitalism. The tension between the ver-tebrate structures of the nation and the cellular logics of flexible capital provides a rich contextual framing of the current politics and global path-ways of migration. This tension characterizes many of the issues and exam-ples raised in the chapters that follow.

The global flow and flexible forms of capital accumulation have led to an expansion of precarious forms of labor that include temporary, short-term, and subcontracted jobs that typically fall outside of forms of state protection (for example, social welfare, insurance, or benefits). At the same time, globalization has also accelerated the increasing erosion of the welfare state, the rise of privatization, and the emphasis on the individual over the collective. The steady expansion of zones of insecure employment has consequently benefited the labor needs of the Global North Atlantic societies (Papadopoulous, Stephenson, and Tsianos, 2008). Other factors like deindustrialization, the economic policies of the Global North, growing inequalities between rural and urban life, militarization, and war have led to massive demographic movement of people from rural to urban areas, and from the Global South to the North.[5] Migrants follow the pathways of capital typically in search of refuge, employment, and the hope of a better life. The very idea of a better life is itself visualized and experienced transnationally, as the chapters in this book will show. The goal here is not to reduce the migration narrative to one that is merely economistic, but rather to emphasize that migration is a dynamic process that shapes, exceeds, and cuts across individuals, communities, economies, nations, and borders. The scholarly challenge is to find the methodological and conceptual stance to capture the intricacies of these intersections.

Changes in immigration policy and control in the Global North inevitably have transnational repercussions. Whether it is deportation, naturalization, asylum policies, or refugee resettlement, all these involve assertions of national sovereignty but have consequences that are felt beyond national borders. For example, in 2010, President Obama signed into law a $600-million Border Bill to pay for border security and surveillance drones on the southwest border of the United States. Under the proposal brought forward by Senator Charles Schumer of New York, the resources for border surveillance were to be paid for by a $2,000 increase on visa fees for temporary skilled workers.[6] In turn, this dealt a financial blow to firms that take advantage of the skilled visa program to bring in temporary skilled workers from India to the United States. While Indian technology outsourcing companies that send thousands of skilled employees to the US raised an outcry and called the bill discriminatory, the bill was applauded by Janet Napolitano, then Secretary of Homeland Security: "It's just a great package."[7] The US legislation controls one form of economic migration in order to clamp down on the porosity of another border. In this manner, the strategy of clamp, control, and containment adds complex transnational twists to both the biopolitical management and political economy of migration. This is but one example of many such global instances. Discussions about refugees and immigrant populations in other parts of the world involve similar shifts between strategic assertions of national sovereignty, transnational institutions, and a cast of private and public actors. For example, African migration to various European countries is being increasingly perceived as a supranational crisis involving not only national borders but Schengen borders as well (Horsti, 2008). As states outsource various functions related to the security, detention, and transportation of undocumented immigrants to corporate control, there has also been a growing trend in the privatization of immigration management.[8] Any study of diasporic publics and spaces should factor in these global considerations, especially how transnational regimes of border control, markets, and cultural institutions together shape and regulate desires, struggles, and practices on the ground.

As the nation-state continues to retain yet modify its sovereign control of populations and their mobility, there are also complex forms of interdependencies between nation-states, diasporas, and transnational institutions. Ong (1999: 16) describes these relations as "complicated accommodations, alliances and creative tensions between the nation-state and mobile capital, between diaspora and nationalism, or between the influx of immigrants and the multicultural state." Both nations and diasporic communities work these tensions, leading to new types of social connections, configurations, and subject positions. Nations reach out to the diaspora and their economic power by offering them various types of financial incentives and access. For example, the government of India has created a special category for its diaspora, termed "non-resident Indian" and commonly referred to as NRI. Through this category and the state's offer of an overseas citizenship of India, the nation attracts financial investment from its diaspora, privileging especially its middle-class skilled and entrepreneurial migrants (van der Veer, 2005). Silicon Valley is full of stories of young, cosmopolitan, immigrant entrepreneurs shuttling between Palo Alto, Bangalore, and Taipei, forming globally distributed entrepreneurial networks (Saxenian, 2006), and exemplifying new modes of subject-making valorized by the logics of neoliberal globalization (Ong, 1999). Similarly, in the Philippines, for example, both the state and corporate actors are highly invested in the diaspora, both for their remittances and for their spending power as consumers. The cultivation of consumer subjectivity boosts the neoliberal agenda by serving both the market and the state's market-based agenda (Padios, 2011). In rapidly growing economies like India, the diaspora serves an important economic and symbolic function in the assertion of a global and cosmopolitan national identity (Koshy and Radhakrishnan, 2008). Nations strategically and selectively include citizens and immigrants who serve as nodes in the flow of capital and as key players in the scripts of a highly mediated global modernity, a theme that will be explored in this book, particularly in the conclusion.

Diasporic communities and nations also leverage transnational locations to influence national politics and reinforce allegiance. Vertovec (2009) argues that overseas communities are increasingly engaging themselves in the economic, social, and political life of their country of origin while states try to channel this engagement to their own advantage. For example, in the year 2000, Vincente Fox actively campaigned among Mexicans living in the United States to support his bid for presidency.[9] Even though in most cases, they cannot vote from abroad, immigrant communities are considered an important group exerting considerable influence on their social networks back home. As early as in 1990, the Irish president Mary Robinson identified herself in her inaugural speech as leader of "the extended Irish family abroad," asserting that "the State is not the only model of community that Irish people can and do identify."[10] Other groups like the diasporic Sri Lankan Tamils, Kurds, and Uyghurs have all made different types of interventions into national politics using global and digital forms of networking and communication. At the same time, there continues to be a deep disjuncture between these transnational modes of political subjectivity and nation-based forms and expectations of citizenship.

In the state formulations of citizenship articulated in naturalization ceremonies, there is the formal requirement of a severing of one's previous national affiliations and transference of loyalty to the adopted nation. The oath of allegiance read at the naturalization ceremony in the United States exemplifies this daunting finality: "I hereby declare, on oath, that I absolutely and entirely renounce and abjure all allegiance and fidelity to any foreign prince, potentate, state, or sovereignty, of whom or which I have heretofore been a subject or citizen."[11] Yet paradoxically, newly naturalized citizens often have a host of social, political, and even banal reasons to acquire a different citizenship. The reasons might extend from gaining safety in a new locale to the ease of travel with a United States passport or sponsoring family members back home, or to other entrepreneurial needs. Under the conditions of a connected global world, naturalized citizenship is not only about establishing new loyalties; it often enables and facilitates existing national affiliations, connections, and travel. As an asylum applicant cited by Coutin (2013: 511) states, "the day that I receive (legal permanent residency) papers, that very day, I'm catching a plane to go to El Salvador again. It's been 11 years since I've seen my parents." To many immigrants, naturalization and the ritual of renunciation of ties enable, ironically, the possibilities of maintaining global networks of local connections. These layers of contradiction, complicated by media technologies, serve as the contextual backdrop for the discussions that follow. The topography of migrant life today refuses containment and is entangled, spread out, and dispersed transnationally.

## Migration and Mediations

The 2014 prizewinning entry in the World Press Photo contest, "Signals" by John Stanmeyer, captures the silhouettes of men under a deep-blue night sky raising their glowing cell phones skyward to catch a signal. According to one of the jurors, "It's a photo that is connected to so many other stories – it opens up discussions about technology, globalization, migration, poverty, desperation, alienation, humanity."[12] The men in Stanmeyer's visual composition are standing on the shore of the Red Sea on a moonlit night in Djibouti City, a stop-off point for migrants in transit from countries such as Ethiopia, Somalia, and Eritrea. Stanmeyer calls this image, "a picture of hope" that shows "that natural desire of needing to connect is universal in all of us." There is indeed a haunting quality to the image, and it is a scene that is being replayed in many global locations, as migrants anxiously navigate their passage across borders.

While the photographer's theory about the universal expression of connection is indeed true on some level, there are raw particularities that are inscribed in those silhouettes of migrants holding their digital devices. To cautiously balance any quick claim of universality, we need to think about the hidden narratives that exceed the frame of the photograph. In a powerful argument, Azoulay (2008: 14) notes that the photograph constitutes an event and is a source of heterogeneous knowledge: "One needs to stop looking at the photograph and instead start watching it. The verb *to watch* is usually used to regard phenomena or moving pictures. It entails dimensions of time and movement that need to be reinscribed in the interpretation of the still photographic image." Following this critical intervention, let us consider the exclusions and negations that underwrite this powerful image by Stanmeyer. What social, political exigencies and personal journeys brought these migrants to this geographical location facing the Red Sea? What are the countries and borders they have traversed already and how many more are there to come before they reach their destinations? What other journeys, trials, or surprises await them? What structural conditions or configurations of violence have led to these migratory journeys and aspirations? What types of connections enable their aspirations and keep them journeying? The cell phone becomes emblematic of their need to connect across borders, to locate themselves and find their bearings in an uncertain environment of risk and impending danger. Yet the very object that may connect them also signals their precarity, their state of being outside the possibility of connection or communication. This photograph is a stark reminder of the politics of mobility, connectivity, and mediation that characterize the contemporary moment.

Mediated practices have always been a part of the immigrant experience and their tenuous relational lives. There has been considerable research on both media representations of immigrants and the ways in which they use media in innovative ways to negotiate cultural space and forge transplanted communities. In fact, scholars studying the media usage of specific diasporic groups have challenged some traditional and territorially rooted ways of understanding media production and reception (e.g. Gillespie, 1995; Cunningham and Sinclair, 2001; Fazal and Tsagarousianou, 2002; Karim, 2002; Bailey, Georgiou, and Harindranath, 2007; Kosnick, 2007). Georgiou (2006: 22), in her study of Greek Cypriots in London and New York, argues that the interactivity and the simultaneity of media enable the diasporic experience to transcend spatial limitations and renew social relations between dispersed homes and transnational positions. Tsagarousianou (2004) notes that diasporic media allows its audiences to produce new spaces where remote localities and diasporic experiences come together. An impressive body of research critically examines the journalistic practices of reporting immigration news and the representation of immigrants, refugees, and asylum seekers in the Western media.[13] The increasing amount of research attention paid to the particularities of different diasporic groups and their media worlds has significantly extended the global base of media studies scholarship.[14] Scholarship on media and migrants enables a more nuanced and differentiated understanding of the media environment, which, as Morley (2000) theorized, has long been premised on the universalist assumption of the dominant and racialized culture of the nation. Arguing for the need to rethink uninterrogated assumptions regarding home and national cultures in the context of global changes, Morley (2000: 3) writes:

> Certainly, traditional ideas of home, homeland and nation have been destabilized, both by new patterns of physical mobility and migration and by new communication technologies which routinely transgress the symbolic boundaries around both the private household and the nation state. The electronic landscapes in which we now dwell are haunted by all manner of cultural anxieties which arise from this destabilizing flux.

These spaces of flux bristle with questions that demand our attention, especially with regard to what Appadurai (1996: 4) terms the "new order of instability in the production of modern subjectivities."

Migration and media have not only to be understood in conjunction, but also to be situated within a global frame. Taken together, globalization and mediation, in Naficy's (2007: xiv) words, constitute a "Janus-faced feature of our contemporary times, one necessitating the other." Whether migrants are following the trail of capital to better their lives or leaving politically dangerous situations, migrant lives are embedded in media ecologies that document, archive, entertain, connect, and shape their experiences. In addition, migrants are also subject to elaborate forms of profiling, finger-printing, systems of recognition, and surveillance at borders, immigration checkpoints, and more. New communication modalities, platforms, and practices enable the very possibilities of maintaining familial ties across spatial and temporal divides. These interactive options have reworked the deep ruptures with the homeland that characterized diasporic life in the past. The chapters that follow show how categories such as home, nation, and citizenship have been radically redefined by migrants through their mobility, transnational visibility, and modes of connection.

New technologies enable both the disciplining and self-expression of migrant communities worldwide. Devices, technologies, and various types of changing media platforms are being widely used by migrants to reinvent and redefine identity. More visibly, in ethnic neighborhoods in cities like New York, Los Angeles, London, Toronto, or Berlin, local entrepreneurs stock a motley selection of commodities that cash in on migrant nostalgia and longing for the homeland. It is common to see ethnic stores selling an assortment of things including movies, music, phone cards, luggage, *balik-bayan* boxes, and gadgets in different voltages for use in various countries. There are almost always money-exchange centers transferring money to relatives and family back home. In short, there is a visible predominance of media objects and communication technologies that redefine the terms of connection with the homeland and bridge the affective distances in immigrant lives. Satellite dishes, for example, are a characteristic sight in ethnic neighborhoods. These technologies of connectivity remap local spaces anew as globally connected hubs. Displaced populations and migrants who have always, of necessity, been media savvy (see Naficy, 2007) now use blogs, social media, chat rooms, YouTube, Twitter, and mobile apps to connect to the various "elsewheres" in their lives and navigate different experiential terrains. For example, I received an invitation to a wedding in India that listed the time of the wedding in three international time zones, providing handy information for diasporic relatives and friends to tune in via Skype technology for the ceremony. The elaborate wedding ceremony and the performance of the rituals are often radically redesigned as a media spectacle. This enables the extended family in the diaspora to be involved, have a visual experience via technology, and participate in real time. Diasporic events are shared in the same way with distant relatives.

Everything from weddings to raising children or learning to cook traditional dishes is now becoming mediated transnational social experience, using digital technologies. By industry accounts, it is immigrants who make the most video calls with smartphones.[15] The range of communication plat-forms designed for, against, and about migrants is endless – ranging from mobile apps giving out the best times to cross the border, video games on nabbing immigrants without papers, and tracking apps to vlogging, GPS, and tracking devices. The diversity of communication channels and plat-forms has been integrated into all aspects of immigrant life. The vast and seemingly borderless space of the Internet offers possibilities for immigrant groups to network. In fact, Diminescu (2008) and Diminescu and Loveluck (2014) argue that the paradigmatic figure of the uprooted migrant is yield-ing to the figure of the connected migrant who, due to the availability of diverse communication devices and channels, simultaneously straddles two sociocultural worlds. One could easily venture a guess that transnational migrants today balance more than two worlds.

Given that the electronic space of media and the space of sociality are already deeply interconnected (Couldry and McCarthy, 2004), the con-figuration of multiple linked worlds in migrant lives offers some interesting global inflections. There has been considerable interest among scholars from different disciplines in examining how these connections are shaped and managed by transnational communities through the use of information and communication technologies (Panagakos and Horst, 2006). In a rich ethno-graphic analysis of transnational parenting, migration, and media practices, Madianou and Miller (2012) propose the new term *polymedia* to capture the plurality of options and choices that characterize the new communica-tive environment. The phenomenon now being termed *digital diaspora* and the role of information communication technologies in the lives of immi-grants have gained considerable research attention (see Brinkerhoff, 2009; Alonso and Oiarzabal, 2010; Fortunati, Pertierra, and Vincent, 2013). This focus on the mediated practices of transnational communities adds a digital twist to the notion of imagined communities that, earlier, Anderson (1991) notably argued were shaped by the power of print capitalism. The research on digital diaspora extensively covers the use of various types of technologies and the ways in which websites, chat groups, web pages, blogs, and social media promote diverse types of connections, discussions, interventions, and activism. For example, the use of cell phones, according to Vertovec (2004), acts as social glue binding transnational migrants to their families; at other times, it enables the transnational coordination of social life (Horst, 2006). Engagement via Internet forums and social media activism influ-ences nationalist politics in the homeland (Bernal, 2006; Shichor, 2010). Other research shows that accessibility and usage continue to be predicated on class, language skills, and immigration status (Mitra, 2001; Benítez, 2006). Gajjala (2010) cautions that scholars should interrogate the term *digital diaspora* and be wary of its celebratory connotations. For instance, ethnographic work with asylum seekers in Germany showed that access or proximity to digital media spaces does not automatically suggest connectivity, since complex emotions like shame, threat, and self-censorship keep some refugees, especially women, from making connections (Witteborn, 2014). The links to home are digitally possible but tenuous and complicated in actuality. For example, it is a common sight to see young men who are part of the large South Asian migrant labor force in the United Arab Emirates taking digital pictures of themselves against the backdrop of beautiful buildings to send to their families back home. In a casual conversation, a South Asian man taking pictures along the Corniche in Abu Dhabi told me that he and his friends always send pictures of themselves in front of imposing buildings in order to hype up the luster of living overseas, in contrast to the reality of their stark existence in the labor camps.[16] To young, stranded immigrants in Ethiopia who connect with their relatives abroad via Skype or Facebook, these forms of communication serve as their only affective capital while in limbo (Leurs, 2014). Ponzanesi and Leurs (2014: 7) make an important and insightful comment: "digital connectedness does not come as a utopian alternative to histories of dislocation, rejection and expulsion." This reminder is especially important in the race to study new and newer digital media. The preoccupation with the newness and the present often eschews complex histories, resulting in the tendency to both reify media objects and essentialize cultures.

Narratives of movement and communication are braided into the migrant experience, which, we should stress, is by no means a singular or totally universal experience. In the 1956 novel about migrants *The Lonely Londoners*, Selvon (1956: 26) writes poignantly about the bustling scene in Waterloo whenever a boat-train arrives in London with passengers from Trinidad. Even immigrants who have lived in Britain long enough still find themselves going to the station, according to Selvon, just hoping to meet someone they might know from the past:

> "Aye Watson! What the hell you doing in Brit'n boy? Why you didn't write me you was coming?" And they would start big old talk with the travellers, finding out what happening in Trinidad, in Grenada, in Barbados, in Jamaica and Antigua, what is the latest calypso number, if anybody dead, and so on, and even asking strangers questions they can't answer, like they know Tanty Simmons who living Labasse in Port of Spain or a feller name Harrison working in the Red House.

It is poignant that these working-class Caribbean immigrants waited in Waterloo station for no one in particular. They were there to catch up through word of mouth about the latest happenings, and get news about people and events back home. The public space of the station served as the meeting place for the immigrants coming to London from the colonies. The station represented the place of arrivals and departures, always evoking mixed emotions. In the 1950s, Waterloo station was becoming a British counterpart of New York's Ellis Island[17] – the place where the reality of the new elsewhere hits and traps immigrants, like the ones in Selvon's world. In contrast, today's migrants catch up with families through a variety of communication channels whose infrastructures assure instant contact, thereby changing not just the nature of communication but the experience of migration. In Adichie's (2013: loc. 6) novel *Americanah*, the central character, Ifemelu, a Princeton-educated African immigrant, writes a lifestyle blog. In her moments of "amorphous longings, shapeless desires, brief imaginary glints of other lives she could be living," Ifemelu turns to the Internet:

> She scoured Nigerian websites, Nigerian profiles on Facebook, Nigerian blogs, and each click brought yet another story of a young person who had recently moved back home, clothed in American or British degrees, to start an investment company, a music production business, a fashion label, a magazine, a fast-food franchise. She looked at photographs of these men and women and felt the dull ache of loss, as though they had pried open her hand and taken something of hers. Nigeria became where she was supposed to be, the only place she could sink her roots in without the constant urge to tug them out and shake off the soil.

Unlike Selvon's immigrants who thronged together in Waterloo station, Ifemelu's migration narrative is shaded by the neoliberal economy and discourses of lifestyle, fast food, brands, and a revised dream of the return. Ifemelu represents a different type of African immigrant, "well fed and watered but mired in dissatisfaction," and fleeing not from war but "from the oppressive lethargy of choicelessness" (Adichie, 2013: loc. 4671). Stereotypical images of migrants from Africa are typically of those fleeing from war or extreme poverty, but Adichie captures the burgeoning middle class of Lagos with its global aspirations, conditioned "to look towards somewhere else, eternally convinced that real lives happened in that somewhere else" (Adichie, 2013: loc. 4671). Both these sets of class-based immigrant experiences, from Selvon and Adichie respectively, serve as historical snapshots that represent shared, yet distinct experiences of mobility and sociality. They also demonstrate how the political, social, and communication infrastructures shape and mediate the nature of transnational connections forged between the migrant, the nation, and the realities of dislocations and relocations.

Sociological research on migration has historically privileged assimila-tionist models where old worldviews are assumed to be shed or overcome and exchanged in a linear or developmental manner. These models of change rely on static and essentialist notions of culture, which in an age of global flows are not only reductive but utterly anachronistic as well. As they strive to emplace themselves in new global locations, migrants find inno-vative and resilient ways of maintaining cross-border connections. These transnational modes of reinventing everyday performances are intricately linked to mediated practices and reveal what de Certeau (1984: xv) calls "the dispersed, tactical and make-shift creativity of groups or individuals already caught in the nets of 'discipline'." As mentioned earlier, this book does not set out to elaborate on the properties of a particular platform, reify or celebrate the impact of specific digital artifacts or technologies. Rather my goal is to show how social and mediated practices meet in the lives and political contestations of transnational migrants. The term *mediation* has been discussed and debated in great detail by media scholars.[18] Here in these chapters, the term arises primarily to highlight the constitutive and transformatory role of media in the cultural and social life of migrants in the context of globalization. Silverstone in his influential work on media theory describes mediation as a "fundamentally, but unevenly, dialectical process in which institutional communication (the press, the broadcast radio and television, and increasingly the world wide web), are involved in the gen-eral circulation of symbols in social life" (Silverstone 2002: 762). Building on this notion of mediation, with a view to making it more theoretically supple, Couldry (2008) argues that it might be more productive to think about mediation as capturing a variety of dynamics within media flows. In addition, he notes: "We need not assume any 'dialectic' between particular types of flow, still less need we assume any stable circuit of causality; we must allow not only for non-linearity but for discontinuity and asymme-try" (Couldry, 2008: 381). The mediated migrant experiences described here reflect these discontinuities and asymmetries. Not only do the fields of media and migration mutually complicate each other, but their intersec-tion, as the chapters that follow describe, invites a rethinking of categories and assumptions from a transnational perspective. The subject of migration presents an opportunity to expand the scope and study of media – its pres-ence, forms, and practices in everyday life. As Mazzarella (2004: 345) not-ably points out, the question of globalization should push scholars to "think more carefully not simply about media but also, and more generally, about mediation as a constitutive process in social life."

## Text: Point of View and Flow

The chapters that follow engage with the cultural politics of migration as a site of innovation, tension, and contestation. The massive global demographic shifts that constitute immigration today represent the circulatory currents of our times. Yet migration is not about the complete freedom to move. Migrant mobility is a site of restriction and control, regulated by assertions of governmental surveillance and national power. To the migrants, it is about grappling with the various challenges that come with facing mobility and immobility, negotiating social networks, and finding one's moorings in new spaces. To those who perceive themselves as rightful natives, immigration conjures up the presence of Others, those who unsettle and interrupt the narrative of a homogenous nationalism. Since the space of immigration control has also become increasingly militarized, levels of fear are being routinely ratcheted up and spread among the public at large. While migrants continue to be regarded as a source of contamination, they constitute both a large labor force across the class structure and a growing consumer niche for the global market. For instance, bodies that are not welcome as citizens still continue to be in demand as temporary labor and as consumers. *Mediating Migration* addresses how these complex intersections that span global locations are imagined, performed, and reproduced in our highly media-saturated times.

In order to engage with cultural politics, Grossberg (1993: 90) argues for radical contextualization, which involves "the work of placing particular practices into particular relations or context, and of transforming one set of relations, one context, into another." This contextual emphasis is a reminder to study migration as complex, multi-layered processes that are inextricably linked to shifting lines of power. By virtue of its transnational fluidities, migration demands this global contextualization, within which the mediation of everyday lives is constituted. For instance, in July 2014, there were angry outbursts in the US about the arrival of undocumented children from Central America who had made the dangerous trek across multiple countries to the US border at Texas, Arizona, or California. One anti-immigrant protestor in Oracle, Arizona, told a reporter: "I am protesting the invasion of the United States by people of foreign countries. This is about the sovereignty of our nation."[19] In Murrieta, California, anti-immigrant groups protesting the *invasion* of the United States managed to keep the Department of Homeland Security buses carrying undocumented children from entering the town where the children were to be processed by federal agents. Meanwhile, pro-immigration protestors carried posters saying, "No human is illegal" or

"Racism is not patriotism." The conversation about citizenship, both in the United States and in Europe, is changing dramatically with the rising numbers of migrants and the mounting animosity toward them. It is also widely recognized that migrants across the board, from the highly skilled to those on the fringes, and their everyday cultures add to the economic and cultural vibrancy of global cities (Georgiou, 2014). It is within these overlapping and colliding discursive frames that we need to contextualize the different types of mediations and meaning-making about migration.

In order to grapple with the tensions inherent in the space of migration, Brah (1996: 16), writing about the South Asian experience in Britain, proposed the notion of diaspora space to foreground the "entanglement of genealogies of dispersion with those of staying put." The concept of diaspora space, according to Brah, decenters binaries such as native/immigrant and insider/outsider, and draws attention to the performative and distributed sites of power. To draw out its critical potentialities further, this diasporic space can be viewed as a mediated transnational space in order to texture our contextual understanding of the particularities of migrant subjectivity and locations. The fact that diasporic life is fully ensconced and scripted within mediated worlds is also sparking some interesting trends. The thriving Bollywood film industry of India, for example, draws heavily on the economy of desire and geographical dispersal of the South Asian diaspora. In charting its global growth, the film industry relies heavily on the diaspora's geographical presence, cultural involvement, and participation in the nation (see Punathambekar, 2005). The musical culture of Bollywood films and its rapidly converging media environment spreads into the social life of the diaspora, including the wedding industry and fashion, thereby consolidating the converging cultures of consumerism that connect the nation and the diaspora. This book tracks the tangled politics of such mediated connections, transnational circulations, and linkages.

Engaging with issues and questions concerning the intersection of media, communication, and migration, the chapters that follow take into consideration overlapping contextual factors. The chapters discuss a variety of specific contexts and practices that concern (1) the performative politics of global mobility; (2) mediated reinventions of transnational cultures; and (3) the emergence of new publics who are demanding and defining forms of visibility through their social, political, and cultural practices. The chapters, developed as distinct but related essays, all respond to current events, crises, and political demands around immigration – the pressing, hot-button topic of our time. This approach enables an examination of the dynamic social processes that characterize the mediated diasporic space. The chapters are organized around some key themes that frame discussions of culture, media, and migration, which I describe briefly in what follows, highlighting the rationale that drives the development and flow of the chapters.

War, militarization, terrorism, and geopolitical conflicts have created high levels of public suspicion about bodies that don't belong, bodies that are perceived as being out of place.[20] The next two chapters of the book focus on issues that have particular contemporary resonance – the questions of legitimacy and recognition of the migrant subject. State vigilance at the border has created "an abject diaspora – a deportspora" (Nyers, 2003: 1070). These migrants with no documents or status are raising their voices in various parts of the world and challenging normative notions of citizenship. In 2006, undocumented migrants organized record-breaking protests in major American cities leading up to a general strike, called "A day without immigrants," leading the *New York Times* to describe the events as a "miracle of grassroots mobilization that turned a shadow population into a national movement in less than a month."[21] With vibrant organizing and the active use of social media, the undocumented movement in the United States has initiated a serious conversation about rights, status, and citizenship. Using the language of coming out, the activists merge different types of subaltern positions and politics. The discussion in chapter 2 weaves together the innovative media activism of the Dreamers and the high-profile coming out of Jose Antonio Vargas to show how undocumented communities are collectively redefining the meaning of citizenship. Through energetic mobilizing, the undocumented migrants represented in this chapter are actively creating digital archives of their own hidden biographies. In the manner described powerfully by Rancière (2004: 226), their activism makes visible what had been excluded and makes audible what used to be inaudible.

Fears over new immigrant groups are often extensions of older prejudices. The media play a major role in the circulation and escalation of these anxieties. In 2012, a white supremacist, Wade Page, fatally shot six people in a Sikh temple in Wisconsin. Speculations ran high in the media that this was a case of a misdirected hate crime, that Page might have shot the Sikhs because in his ignorance he thought they were Muslims. It is true that since the terrorist attacks on September 11, 2001, members of the Sikh community, all across the United States, have been the victims of hate crimes. In the Orientalist merging of turbans, beards, and religions, all brown faces seem to disappear into undifferentiated anonymity. However, this type of speculation about misdirected crime is based on some very problematic assumptions. It seems to suggest that were Wade Page to have committed this act of violence in a mosque against Muslims, somehow, given the climate of Islamophobia, "such a crime would be more explicable, more easily rationalized, less worthy of moral outrage."[22] There have been a number of cases of mistaken identity over the years, which have complex racial underpinnings. In chapter 3, I engage with these issues and a specific case of mistaken identity when a young, missing South Asian college student was misidentified as being the Boston Marathon bomber by overzealous digital publics. The politics of recognition takes unexpected twists in the crowd-sourced court of social media.

Next, in chapter 4, I turn to the gendered subject of transnationality, the Islamic practice of veiling, and the contestations about what constitutes communication and civil engagement in the secular public sphere. Public discourse distinguishes the citizen from the immigrant Other, by evoking a deep cultural divide between what are perceived as anachronistic traditions associated with migrants and the practices of liberal modernity. Using a statement made about Muslim women's veiling by Jack Straw, a well-known British public figure, as a point of departure, this chapter elaborates on the complex ways in which the performative demands of being publicly modern are being defined in the contemporary global context. Debates over modernity and tradition are staged over women's eyes and bodies, bringing the gendered Islamic subject of transnationality into public focus and simultaneously rendering her inadmissible. What does this say about the assumptions that guide our normative understanding of what constitutes effective communication?

Chapters 5 and 6 move into the performative space of food, music, and the forging of cultural communities. Both chapters address different ways in which digital media has become a part of the everyday lives of immigrants. Specifically, drawing on my own subject location and ethnographic experiences, I discuss how the South Asian diaspora actively connects and communicates with the homeland, questioning, disrupting, and pushing the bounds of belonging and identity. The labor of preserving the authenticity of traditions has historically (and often problematically) been relegated to women and closely associated with the differentiation of the private and public domains of activity. Now the binary of private and public has been blurred in the neoliberal context, where the market potentialities of tradition itself are being mined. In chapter 5, I turn to these issues from the perspective of South Asian women who blog about food to stay connected to familiar culinary practice and familial networks. In the intimacy of the virtual kitchen, the women bloggers create a global culinary archive that mines regional details and local origins, only to go beyond and forge transnational culinary publics. However, here too in these liquid spaces of blogs and memes, there are borders between tastes, bodies, and communities that, as I show in this chapter, appear both in the text and algorithmically.

Continuing the discussion of portable traditions in the diasporic context, chapter 6 showcases how immigrant communities from southern India preserve Carnatic music, a very esoteric style of Indian classical music in the United States. The Internet and communication platforms like Skype are offering new possibilities for the diaspora to connect performatively with the nation. This diasporic desire to reconnect with classical traditions leads to a concomitant globalization of the art form itself. This chapter argues that new diasporic cultural formations are being constituted as digital cultures reorganize the sensory landscape of globalization. This leads into a discussion of aura in a transnational context, when the performer and the performance are taken out of the original national setting and fidelity is reproduced through technological means. The diasporic space introduces a global perspective and complicates the discussion of authenticity – a key concept in media studies. These two chapters on food and music also address how the diaspora becomes a consumer niche for the market economy and a resource for the nation, in this case, a globalizing India.

In the concluding chapter, I return to the articulation and performance of power in contestations over documents, identities, space, and the economy. Historically, societies have resisted the arrival of immigrants, who were thought to infect the environment or pose an economic burden or threat. These old resentments are reappearing with regularity, directed to newer groups, moving along different pathways, coded in mediated terms, under the powerful influence of the neoliberal economy. There are no simple binaries and singular categories that can explain the complex experiential pathways of migrant experiences. These life worlds and social fields push the limits of our imagination and force us to think globally and inclusively. The pages that follow are an exercise in this direction.

# 2    Legitimacy:
##       Accumulating Status

> We owe them for having broken through the communication barriers, for being seen and heard for what they are: not specters of delinquency and invasion, but workers and families, from here and there at the same time, with their particularisms and the universality of their condition as modern proletarians.
>
> Balibar, 2000: 42

The voices and activism of undocumented immigrants, variously termed irregular migrants, non-citizens, or the sans-papiers, are radically transforming normative understandings of citizenship and belonging. As casualties of colonial histories, economic globalization, and militarization, increasing numbers of people are placed in impossible situations contending with the complex demands of crossing borders. Without documents or status, their claims for inclusion and very presence within the nation-state have precipitated public reengagement with discourses of belonging and unleashed widespread anxiety about the nation coming apart at its cultural seams. From the standpoint of the nation-state, the undocumented are perceived as intruders who have broken the law and hence can neither exercise any rights nor expect any privileges normally afforded to citizens. However, far from being specters of delinquency and invasion (Balibar, 2000), the undocumented are fully immersed as civic participants in the social and economic life of the nation. It is precisely this tension and its consequences that make them stand out as anomalies with respect to dominant narratives of citizenship (Soysal, 1995: 2).

The complex trajectories of immigrant lives unsettle the idea of a transparent and singular mode of affiliation to a nation-state or political community. Balancing their transnational social connections and a fluid sense of home, undocumented immigrants confront the precarity of their status in the most mundane routines of everyday life. The messy entanglements that define the existential realities faced by irregular or non-status immigrants disrupt the conventional lines demarcating the categories of insider and outsider. What role do these terms serve today and how are they mobilized to various ends? The rigid binaries of "us" and "them," according to Kapur (2005: 109), "undermine the human rights of the transnational migrant subject and fail to address the complex, fragmented, and blurred realities of our transnational world." Surviving beneath the radar of state sovereignty, the undocumented live with the constant fear of deportation and of being wrenched away from their families and familiar surroundings. At the same time, as seen in various immigrant protests worldwide,[1] the undocumented are finding ways to redefine their dispossession and attach themselves to the nation that does not recognize them. The performative, as Butler and Athanasiou (2013: loc. 1734) argue, "emerges precisely as the specific power of the precarious – unauthorized by existing legal regimes, abandoned by the law itself – to demand the end to their precarity."

The dramatic nature of protests by those granted no political legitimacy is transformed very quickly into highly visible media events. On May 28, 2013, a small group of people gathered in the public arena of Union Square in New York City for the fourth annual Coming out of the Shadows event,[2] a nationwide event galvanized by social media and organized specifically for undocumented youth. I went to this busy New York City space to hear young people share stories about their vulnerable situation and "unauthorized" status. Wearing T-shirts with the slogan "Undocumented and Unafraid," they took the microphone and related their stories of survival. Some declared their status loudly and others held back tears, speaking about how they live under the constant fear and threat of deportation. The crowd applauded, showing their support and appreciation for the young people and their cause.[3] The rally, by providing a face for the issue, humanized the debate about borders and raised moral and ethical issues concerning the condition of being undocumented. One young university student declared at the rally in Union Square:

> Our undocumented status does not define us. Our undocumented status does not tell us how good a person we are. Because we are individuals, we are Americans. We've been in America for many years. So you can't tell me I'm *just* an undocumented student. I'm an American. (Flanders, 2013)

A few yards away from where I stood listening to the speakers, another, much smaller, angrier anti-immigration group stood resolutely in defense of the US border. Members of the group, New Yorkers for Immigration Control and Enforcement, held banners with the words, "No Trespassing" and "Secure our Borders." Bystanders gathered to watch as an altercation took place between members of the two groups about the subject of legality, borders, and amnesty. One member of the anti-immigrant group stated his position unequivocally: "Without walls, you don't have a society." In turn, a pro-immigration supporter retorted loudly with these rather profound words: "The tide of history is against you guys."

Struggles over citizenship and its meanings, such as this one in Union

Square, are indeed intricately tied to the tides of history. The presence and mobility of irregular and undocumented migrants are deeply connected to the flows of global capital, its incessant demand for disposable labor, and its disruptive impact on societies. Migrants, in turn, are forced to find innovative ways of navigating the complex transnational terrain and repercussions of restrictive immigration controls. Yet the undocumented, an abject class of global migrants, are perceived either as victims or as objects of fear possessing "unsavory agency (i.e. they are identity-frauds, queue jumpers, people who undermine consent in the polity) or a dangerous agency (i.e., they are criminals, terrorists, agents of insecurity)" (Nyers, 2003: 1070). Challenging that stereotypical perception, the protestors in Union Square gathered in solidarity to contest their precarious status, using the power of their visibility and voice, both of which ironically are not recognized by the state. When the young woman in Union Square boldly declares that her undocumented status does not define her, she is publicly evoking and refusing her unauthorized position. The lack of status is now used to ignite a new politics of citizenship. This moment of defiance represents "the intertwined bodily and spatial quality of not-giving-up as not-giving-in" (Butler and Athanasiou, 2013: loc. 393). Through their activism and persistence, the protestors seem intent on opening up a much larger discussion about identity and demanding a more humane nationalism that exceeds conventional assumptions about the nation and its obligations. In fact, commenting on the immigration situation in France, Balibar (2000: 43) writes that the wider national community owes the sans-papiers a debt for giving politics a new life and for the re-creation of citizenship "in as much as it is not an institution or a statute but a collective practice."

In reality, however, the discourse of securitization and the aggressive tactics employed by the state to police the nation's borders have led to the increased criminalization of undocumented immigrants (De Genova, 2005; Coutin, 2011; Inda, 2005). The immigrant body as a threat to the safety of the nation is deeply embedded in the punitive gaze and governance practices of the state. Since the terrorist events that occurred in New York, London, and Madrid, these disciplinary regimes, zealously supported in the name of patriotism, have produced what Behdad (2005: 10) terms "popular forms of vigilantism" creating an intensely hostile anti-immigrant environment. In the dominant discourse, undocumented migrants represent the chaotic and illegitimate movement of people who are testing and wearing out the resources of the nation, which stands in contrast to the legitimate movement of those considered to be "a productive force to be harnessed or managed" (Squire, 2011: 3). Since their constitutive role in the political order is predicated on their exclusion and unauthorized presence (Astor, 2009), the undocumented lack both the rights and the ability to express themselves politically. In the contemporary context, with increasing numbers of people forced to move between national borders, scholars argue that irregularity should be treated not as a fixed status or a singular experience (Coutin, 2005), but rather as a condition that "immigrants and citizens move in and out of depending on whether their movements and activities are targeted for control by national, international and/or transnational agencies" (Squire, 2011: 8). Hence instead of representing irregularity as an absolute end of rights, status, and mobility (Nyers, 2010), it is more productively viewed as the condition constituted and produced by the technologies and global politics of border control and mobility. How do subjects become political actors and claimants of rights in contexts where they are not recognized? Isin (2008: 18) suggests shifting our attention to acts of citizenship or to maintain "a focus on those moments when, regardless of status and substance, subjects constitute themselves as citizens – or better still, as those to whom the right to have rights is due."

## Revisioning Citizenship

The exclusionary paradigm of citizenship serves as the provocative focal point of the demonstrations of undocumented immigrants. Since the early 2000s, the activism of undocumented immigrants has strongly opposed the fixity of state-centric notions of citizenship and exposed their assumptions as untenable or even anachronistic in the current global context. In 2003, in a remarkable show of strength, drawing their inspiration from the civil rights movement, migrant workers from ten cities across the US converged on Washington DC to assert their presence and demand their rights as workers. In 2006, more than 3,000,000 immigrants protested in the streets of Chicago, Denver, Los Angeles, Phoenix, and several other cities across the United States for comprehensive immigration reform. In a move that surprised the nation and the world, immigrants delivered a message to Capitol Hill: "We are workers and neighbors, not criminals."[4] Through the sheer strength and orchestration of their collective presence, undocumented immigrants emerged as an energetic constituency resisting the conditions that framed them as outsiders and criminals.

Immigrant protests are being noticed as a serious force in the global public sphere. In the United States, in 2013, roughly 11,000,000[5] migrants were grappling with the politics of legality and visibility. In other countries, including Italy, Spain, Greece, and France, according to Tyler and Marciniak (2013: 143), immigrant protests are "exposing the violence engendered by border controls, and challenging the abstract and fetishized political rhetoric of 'illegal immigration'."[6] Designing innovative ways to reinscribe their positions, migrants are dealing with the risks of deportation and claiming legitimacy for themselves within a national structure that does not recognize them. This activism, spurred by the desire to be recognized, is perceived by many to be outright audacious or even an absurd misunderstanding of the relationship of the state to its rightful citizens. Quite frequently the phrase "Which part of the word illegal do you not understand?" pops up on websites and in everyday discourse in connection with this subject (see Vargas, 2012a). The self-evident manner in which this question is posed is clearly related to the high degree of moral consensus about the meaning of citizenship and the normative understandings of what civic engagement means in the public imaginary. Nationalism is reproduced through the maintenance of these social hierarchies and the surveillance of boundaries between rightful and unauthorized bodies. Undocumented immigrants become legible within the polity only by virtue of their precarity, lack of legal authorization, and status. Jayal (2013) argues that beneath the apparently consensual concept of citizenship lies a series of tensions that are expressed in the form of morally loaded binaries, such as good and bad citizenship, active and passive citizenship, or thin and thick citizenship. Distinguishing thin citizenship as legal status and thick citizenship as the more engaged practice and valued performance of citizenship, Jayal (2013: loc. 1614) notes that for claimants, the question of legal status holds meaning that cannot be captured by the simple distinction between thin and thick dimensions. Thin citizenship or legal status, she notes, is not merely a qualifying threshold for the activity of citizenship (Jayal, 2013: loc. 1614).[7] For undocumented migrants, status itself is a prized accomplishment that promises to open doors of security and sociality. Their demands primarily revolve around recognition of their vulnerable existence and gaining access through the technologies of citizenship to the world of work and everyday life.

Resisting state discourses and tactics of border control, undocumented migrants have emerged as activists in the public arena and established themselves as immanent in the structure of the nation. The public narrations of their everyday struggles offer a grassroots revisioning of political participation and citizenship. Undocumented migrants disrupt the naturalized connection between territoriality, citizenship, and belonging by drawing attention to their embodied presence in the nation-state. Their body, as Papastergiadis (2009: 172) argues, is already here and "by being in a place, he or she exists in relation to others." By raising their voices and publicizing their situation, the undocumented bring to the surface a web of social relations, interconnections, and a reality that the nation refuses to recognize. Above all, through their protests, undocumented migrants constitute themselves as a subaltern collective, urging us, as Isin (2002: 3) notes, to rethink citizenship from the perspective of its alterity. In highly transgressive communicative acts that put them at an even greater risk of deportation, these migrants not only are vocal about their vulnerable positions, but also assert themselves as political subjects and articulate demands that have previously been either unspeakable or silenced (De Genova, 2009).

To be able to voice demands and be heard in the public arena has historically been considered the prerogative of citizens included within a paradigm that valorizes a fixed relationship between state, citizen, and territory. As McNevin (2006: 136) writes, "it is only with reference to the state and its citizens as bounded and territorialized identities that the concept of irregular migration is brought into being and that the policing of borders against irregular migrants is justified." Therefore, when irregular or undocumented migrants make claims in a political space where they are regarded as nonentities, their unlikely protests both challenge and expose the limits of a territorialized view of citizenship. Yet, as mentioned earlier, these protests by undocumented migrants are contained within a paradox. On the one hand, the protests are led by players who are considered outsiders in the political equation of the nation. On the other, although removed from the political field defined by the state, undocumented migrants are fully contained within the modalities of border control and state power (Mitropoulous and Neilson, 2006) and created as controllable populations (Papadopoulos and Tsianos, 2013). The undocumented therefore occupy complex positionalities of being both inside and outside of the various regimes of the nation.

The process of governance, or what Rancière (2004) calls the police order, provides coherence to the perception of who is included or excluded, visible or invisible, admissible or inadmissible.[8] Interrupting this consensus happens, in Rancière's view, when those who are not allowed to participate are both seen and heard. "Politics means precisely this, that you speak at a time and in a place you're not expected to speak" (Rancière and Lie, 2006: 5). Undocumented migrants, in the United States today, sometimes known as the Dreamers, are reoccupying their dispossession strategically by making their bodies visible and their voices heard. The Dreamers who are the children of undocumented immigrants form a central piece in the comprehensive immigration reform that has preoccupied the Obama administration. With their lives hanging in a state of limbo with regard to their status, undocumented migrants are finding innovative locations and ways of politicizing the conversation on immigration. With the declaration "unashamed and unafraid," the Dreamers leverage the power and transnational script of their stories. They reboot the discussion on immigration using their state of abjection as "a critical resource in the struggle to rearticulate the very terms of symbolic legitimacy and intelligibility" (Butler, 1993: 3).

In the sections that follow, I turn to this rearticulation and discuss how undocumented migrants expose the exclusionary limits of the American dream and unsettle received discourses about immigration and nationalism. Through the strategic use of communication and social media to circulate their life stories, migrant activists are demanding recognition and asserting their presence through the performance of innovative and resistant modes of citizenship.

## Languaging Bodies

Writing about the contradictions inherent in the immigrant condition, Sayad (2004) states the immigrant is no more than his body. Defined by exclusions and negations, the immigrant is rendered unintelligible and reduced to undifferentiated corporeality. On the subject of the immigrant body, Sayad (2004: 213) writes:

> The importance of what is called the "language of the body," or, to put it a different way, the organic importance of the body, is, basically, nothing more than the importance of the body as organ, or in other words, first as labour power, and only then as a form of self-presentation: the immigrant is primarily his body, his bodily strength and the presence he acquires because he has a biological body that is different from other bodies.

While the bodies of immigrants are disciplined, racialized, and surveilled by regimes of state control, bodies also serve as the main technology of survival for immigrants as they navigate spaces of uncertainty and risk. Marked as an undifferentiated group, undocumented migrants, refugees, and asylum seekers remain "the flotsam and jetsam of the planetary tides of human waste" (Bauman, 2003: 57). They are described as disposable labor, as excess, as intruders, and as an overall source of stress and burden to the nation. The bodies of migrants are routinely caricatured or portrayed in public discourse as deviants who have no place or even as laboring animals. For example, in a fervent and animated opposition to immigration reform, US House Representative Steve King has on several occasions compared immigrants to animals. In 2006, speaking to the House with a prop for his design of a border fence for the US–Mexico border, Steve King advocated the efficacy of adding some electric wiring to the top of the border wall: "We could also electrify this wire with the kind of current that would not kill somebody, but it would be a discouragement for them to be fooling around with it. We do that with livestock all the time" (Legum, 2006). On another occasion, in May 2013, King made the comment that the US should select immigrants in the same way as choosing "the pick of the litter." "You want a good bird dog? You want one that's going to be aggressive? Pick the one that's the friskiest . . . not the one that's over there sleeping in the corner" (Seitz-Wald, 2012). When asked about these comparisons, King, ironically, defended himself by claiming that he was overturning stereotypes, both racial and occupational, about undocumented immigrants and calling for more reciprocity in the relationship between immigrants and the nation. When it came to the Dreamers, King's comments once again focused on their bodies as illegitimate, unwelcome, and out of place in the nation. In reaction to the amount of positive and supportive discourse circulating about young Dreamers, King stated:

> Some of them are valedictorians – and their parents brought them in. It wasn't their fault. It's true in some cases. But they aren't all valedictorians. They weren't all brought in by their parents. For everyone who's a valedictorian, there's another 100 out there who weigh 130 pounds – and they've got calves the size of cantaloupes because they're hauling 75 pounds of marijuana across the desert.[9]

Immigrant-rights advocates responded to King's statements by reappropriating the cantaloupe as a symbol of immigrant dignity and underpaid labor. In a show of solidarity, three activist groups, including United We Dream, America's Voice, and United Farm Workers, came together to deliver cantaloupes to members of Congress who were against immigration reform. Using the cantaloupe as a symbol of immigrant labor to respond to the racism of King's remarks, the activists reached out to Congressional members to persuade them about the need for a more humane policy with regard to young undocumented immigrants. The racist remarks by King provided an opportunity for raising voices and gaining political momentum around immigration reform. The coalition between different immigrant groups such as those working for the Dreamers and the United Farm Workers signified a bridging of issues. As he delivered the cantaloupe to Rep. King's office, Giev Kashkooli of the United Farm Workers said that the cantaloupes were proof of the hard work of hundreds of thousands of immigrants who labor under harsh conditions, harvesting fruits and vegetables to feed the nation. Kashkooli described Rep. King's remarks that the majority of young immigrants are drug runners as both deeply hurtful and flawed: "The racism of his words aren't just words. They animate policies that affect all Americans" (Sarlin, 2013).

The controversy over King's comments and choice of analogies reiterates the fact that the site of immigration is both semantically loaded and politically charged. Words like "amnesty," "illegal," "undocumented," "earned citizenship," and even "cantaloupe" and "calves" were being contested. While reacting to the analogy and describing the arduous labor of harvesting cantaloupes, Kashkooli made repeated references to "new Americans" and shifted the symbolic frame of reference from distorted body images to productive labor. About their hard work, he added: "It's not a workout. It's endured so the rest of the country can enjoy these things" (Sarlin, 2013). In addition to delivering cantaloupes to the seats of power in Washington, Dreamers were posting pictures of their own calves on Twitter under the hashtag #NoCanteloupeCalvesHere. The provocative postings included: "my calves are strong after 2 years of hauling a heavy bag full of Law school books," "my calves are toned from the hours I spend teaching classical ballet," and "my calves are strong from working hard to support our families."[10]

Cantaloupes and calves are reworked as symbols, in order to construct a counter-narrative of nationalism that moved the terms of the debate from legality and boundaries to the contributions of the laboring body of the immigrant. However, King's dubious arithmetic and stereotypical images reiterated the view of immigrants as infiltrators. King specifically differentiates between innocent immigrants who have deep ties to America and those who have been "undermining our culture and civilization and profiting from criminal acts" (Wilstein, 2013). By resurrecting binary categorizations of the good and bad immigrant, King shores up old fears of civilizational contamination and marks certain immigrants as morally unfit for citizenship. Immigrants then are defined, first and foremost, as a problem that has to be curtailed and managed. Yet immigration history has made it very clear that *otherness* plays a vital role in the definition of national belonging. Honig (2001: 4) suggests that we reframe the well-rehearsed question "how should we solve the problem of foreignness?" as "what problems does foreignness solve for us?" The activist campaigns of the Dreamers, and in particular the highly visible outing of the journalist Jose Antonio Vargas, provide a provocative answer to this reframed question about otherness.

## Visible Invisibility

Jose Antonio Vargas, a Pulitzer Prize-winning journalist, is the most recognizable undocumented immigrant in the United States. He has emerged as a key advocate for comprehensive immigration reform, and through his activism has coalesced public support for young undocumented immigrants. Leveraging the potential of social media and an array of platforms to circulate his own biography, Vargas has been very successful in drawing public attention to what he believes is a broken immigration system; fixing it, he claims, requires an inclusive debate and a new national conversation. Through the strategic staging of his life story in his writing, public appearances, campaign website, and even a film, Vargas has been steadily steering the conversation to cover a range of issues about the politics of immigration, deportation, and the very use of the term *illegal* to describe his own status and that of other undocumented immigrants.

Vargas revealed his status as an undocumented immigrant in a 2011 cover story for the *New York Times* magazine. The piece graphically outlined how he came to the United States at the age of 12 to live with his grandparents, accompanied by a smuggler or coyote who, at that time, Vargas mistakenly assumed to be an uncle. It was during a visit to the motor vehicles bureau to get a driver's license that Vargas discovered that his green card was fake. With striking candor, Vargas describes both his life of constant fear and his professional successes, which include bylines in major publications, stories on celebrities like Mark Zuckerberg, and even being part of a *Washington Post* team that won a Pulitzer Prize for the coverage of the 2007 shooting on the campus of Virginia Tech. Trying to stand out and excel only intensified his fear of being found out. Exhausted from the deception and hiding, Vargas decided to tell his story in the article. He also included his experience of coming out as openly gay: "Tough as it was, coming out about being gay seemed less daunting than coming out about my legal status" (Vargas, 2011).

The article went viral, becoming the most-shared piece on Google that month. With the publication of the article, Vargas managed to raise the level of public awareness about what it means to be forever haunted by the fear of being found out, to be part of the undocumented precariat in the United States. By stating that he is now "a walking conversation that most people are uncomfortable having" (Vargas, 2012b), Vargas has been using his visible yet tenuous position to situate the immigration debate within the larger discursive framework of race, sexuality, power, and the economy: "Immigration in the U.S. is more than a question of legality – it's about history, about foreign policy, about economy in a globalized and interconnected world" (Vargas, 2012a). Here is what he writes in the *New York Times* article (Vargas, 2011):

> There are believed to be 11 million undocumented immigrants in the United States. We're not always who you think we are. Some pick your strawberries or care for your children. Some are in high school or college. And some,

it turns out, write news articles you might read. I grew up here. This is my home. Yet even though I think of myself as an American and consider America my country, my country doesn't think of me as one of its own.

Vargas overturns stereotypes, both racial and occupational, about undocumented immigrants and calls for a more reciprocally defined notion of citizenship. He merges thick and thin versions of citizenship, discussed earlier. By identifying himself as globally connected, queer, and loyal, Vargas argues that he and other undocumented immigrants are citizens and Americans in ways that go deeper than papers. With the public declaration of his undocumented status, he disrupts normative expectations and definitions of being a political actor. For example, in February 2013, Vargas presented an emotionally charged statement to the United States Senate Judiciary Committee on Immigration. He stated he and others like him dream of a path to citizenship so that they can actively participate in the American democracy. He emphasized how his lack of immigration status cannot deter his love for the country and concluded with a compelling question:

> Immigration is about our future. Immigration is about all of us and before we take your questions, I have a few of my own: What do you want to do with me? What do you want to do with us? How do you define "American"?[11]

His bold question issued to the seat of political power represents a highly charged demand to reexamine immigration in a climate of resurgent nationalisms and vocal nativism. A few days before the testimony, a Twitter exchange between executive director Mark Krikorian of the conservative Center for Immigration Studies and Vargas was illustrative.

> Illegal alien journalist Jose Antonio Vargas will testify next week before Senate Judiciary. Will anyone arrest him?[12]

Within minutes Vargas tweeted back the words:

> I look forward to seeing you there, Mark. If you want to get me arrested, go ahead. Nothing to fear but fear itself.[13]

Drawing the words of his tweet from the inaugural address of Franklin Delano Roosevelt, Vargas elevates his position, with great economy, from illegal and irrelevant to courageous and near mythical. He appears where he is not supposed to matter or be present. He was seen seated next to the Secretary of Homeland Security during President Obama's January 2013 speech on immigration, and even moderating a White House Fireside Hangout on immigration reform. Commenting in the *Huffington Post* on his situation, Vargas remarked: "It's part of the surreal nature of being an undocumented person in this country . . . You're like visibly invisible."[14]

31

Of threats on tweets

US President Barack Obama after delivering a speech on immigration reform in Las Vegas, January 29, 2013. Jose Antonio Vargas is on the right, facing the president. © Jim Watson/Getty

Vargas and the DREAM activists are gaining public visibility and drawing attention to their predicament. In order to be recognized by the law, they have to engage in highly visible acts that break the law or perform what Isin (2008: 179) terms "acts of irresponsibility." While the undocumented challenge the exclusionary logics of citizenship, their demands stay within the parameters of the system, its registers, and a belief in legalization. Given the vulnerability of their situation, this belief, as De Genova (2009) and others note, is not unusual or surprising.[15] Although powerful, the narration of particular types of life stories circulated by the Dreamers reproduces the exceptionalism of the nation through a reaffirmation of the American Dream. The mystique of the Dream and its conservative center stays intact, and in fact the Dreamers contribute to its reproduction through their digital storytelling.

## Bio-Scripts and Aspirations

The granting of citizenship rests on the state's recognition of eligible bodies. For the Dreamers, biographies serve as primary evidence on which to build a case for their eligibility for citizenship. They claim that they are already constituted as citizens both affectively in terms of their allegiance to the nation, and performatively in terms of their enactments and possession of cultural capital. For instance, in his *New York Times* article and subsequent talks and testimonies, Vargas emphasizes his fluent everyday performance of "Americanness." He mentions his 8th-grade successes in spelling bees, his induction into American pop culture via Michael Jackson and the O. J. Simpson trial, and his immersion in US television programming via popular shows such as *Frasier, Home Improvement,* and reruns of *The Golden Girls.*[16] Vargas and other DREAM rights activists argue that they are not unassimilable cultural outsiders; rather, they claim to possess a badge of citizenship inscribed by a lifetime of growing up in the American everyday with popular culture. Others, including many journalists, politicians, and filmmakers, also view the situation of the Dreamers through the prism of youth and aspirations. They are represented often as young people who have come to the United States under conditions beyond their control. For example, this is how President Obama described the Dreamers in his June 2012 remarks on immigration: "These are young people who study in our schools, they play in our neighborhoods, they're friends with our kids, they pledge allegiance to our flag. They are Americans in their heart, in their minds, in every single way but one: on paper."[17]

Responding to the exclusion and stigmatization they face, undocumented migrants are inserting their words and presence into the logics and exceptionalist mythos of the nation-state. Their campaign has gained considerable energy and momentum mainly through the power of storytelling, and the digital circulation of emotional appeals. Achieving an empathetic response in a climate where the undocumented are perceived as intruders and criminals is not easy. Even a cursory look at the responses to Vargas' article in the *New York Times* reveals the split nature of public opinion on the issue. Judging from the comments and responses to his article, some read it as a story, moving, inspiring, courageous, and honest, others view it as an affront, sinister, shameful, deceitful, and unlawful.[18] Despite the mixed reactions, the stories of the undocumented have emerged in the public domain linking identities explicitly to the space and values of the nation.

In order to both influence impending immigration policy decisions and respond to citizenship requirements of proving residency and character, the Dreamers are intensely preoccupied with the circulation of biographical narratives. Through very savvy use of media, the activists have built an archive of life stories, most of which emphasize the moral standing and worth of undocumented youth hoping to participate in the American Dream. The stories are short diaristic entries that are clearly intended for wide distribution and are constructed to elicit compassion and action from readers or viewers. The stories talk about parental sacrifice, hopes destroyed, facing the reality of a life without documents, shame and living in the shadows. These stories, which have been appearing on a variety of media platforms, including activist websites and anthologies, YouTube clips and documentaries, juxtapose the specter of isolation and the inability to live and dream in the everyday: "I feel like my hands are tied behind my back and I feel unable to take control of my future" (Cyndi, 2012: 22).

Mostly the stories document the exemplary achievements of youngsters who have survived against great odds without status or papers, and have also achieved much in their lives, especially by way of academic success or receiving professional recognition like Vargas. Various immigration activist websites, including Vargas' own Define American.com, have been inviting undocumented youth to post short biographies. The underlying premise is simple: that we need to hear the voice of invisible migrants and read their stories in order to understand their plight. These collections of stories assemble voices that seem to speak in unison about belonging to the country and, among other things, about unfair, inhumane working conditions for immigrants, detention, and forced separation of families.[19] The director of the documentary *Papers* writes, "the barriers that we imagine between us fall away as we hear about these young people's lives in their own words"

(Manuel, Pineda, Galisky, and Shine, 2012). David Guggenheim, the director of the 2013 documentary *The Dream Is Now*, calls for "common sense immigration reform" of a broken immigration policy and presents the lives of four high-achieving Dreamers so that "we can all debate, discuss, and decide for ourselves what is right, what is fair, and what is best for our nation."[20] The website urges you to take action: call, tweet, socialize, dream, write, watch. Repeatedly, we see that the various collections of stories naturalize a "common-sense" understanding that immigrant rights are human rights, thereby establishing the basis on which to build a movement.[21]

This common-sense argument is fortified by the selection and showcasing of portraits of excellence, in the style of Vargas' confessional piece in the *New York Times* described earlier. Senator Dick Durbin of Illinois, the author of the DREAM Act legislation, has presented stories of high-achieving Dreamers to the US Senate and has created a website where more stories can be posted. He tells moving stories of young undocumented immigrants who aspire to be teachers, social workers, nurses, architects, biomedical engineers, lawyers, cancer researchers, musicians, and doctors. He talks of the thwarted ambitions of young people who only want to give back to the country they call home: "they will make America a better, stronger country."[22] It should be noted here that the Senator's website clearly states that passing the DREAM Act will benefit recruitment to the army and will stimulate the economy, and that the Dreamers will not be eligible for federal funds and will be subject to tough criminal penalties for fraud. The possibility of earning legal status is likely for select groups of students with great potential to contribute more fully to America. While the individual successes of the Dreamers are certainly impressive, the lining up of the stories echoes the nationalist agenda, and ultimately excellence is subsumed within the economistic narrative of personal accomplishment. The undocumented are valued only as far as their aspirations can be directly marshaled into the economic structures of capitalism, the securitized gaze of the state, and its pastoral benevolence.

The Dreamer campaign is about the successful generation of small personal stories, particular readings of the American Dream that simultaneously mirror, question, and appropriate the wider national discourses of the country (see Orgad, 2012).[23] In some cases, the stories leverage the personal and the biographical to ask a broader question about moral obligations of citizenry. Jose Vargas' site Define American does not merely solicit Dreamers for their stories, but also appeals to the nation at large to contribute to a definition of America. Clearly the objective seems to be to create a composite of what the nation means and should mean at a time when the terms of mobility and migration have changed. The banner line on the website Define American states the rationale: "When immigrants become U.S. citizens, they swear an oath. We should all be willing to do that. Let's renew our vows to America." The pledge calls for "active Americans" who will "recommit" to the country's creed and "claim America" by pledging to be a citizen whatever one's country of birth might be.[24] The renewed and re-sworn American is the one nominated to engage with this reworked notion of citizenship, where labor, presence, and commitment constitute the basis to claim citizenship.

Vargas and the DREAM activists bring other citizens ("everyday immigration allies") to the movement: "Some are driven by a biblical call to social justice, while others believe this is a moral imperative. They, like Harriet Tubman and countless brave Americans before them, are willing to take personal risks in order to do what is right. These heroes need to be the center of this national conversation. Together, we are going to fix a broken system."[25] Through this persuasive rhetorical move, Vargas lays down the requirements for what constitutes an engaged public. In doing so, he legitimizes the model of the citizen as a proactive individual and entrepreneurial agent (see Brown, 2005; Ong, 2006). This support becomes necessary, as the system does not recognize the contributions of those without papers. The test of patriotism inherent in the famous "ask what you can do for your country" is now rearticulated by the Dreamers to have the following logic: I have done my all for my country, but my country does not recognize me.

## Circulatory Politics

Through multimodal storytelling and the creation of a digital ecology around immigration activism, the DREAM activists have constructed a visible public identity for themselves. First, through the circulation of their narratives and the assertion of their voices as participants in democratic dialogue, they have challenged the dominant view of the undocumented as a threat and burden on the system. Second, the use of technology has both scaled up and added momentum to the conversation. The stories appear and reappear in various mediated formats, reiterating the agenda and circulating the appeals embedded in the narratives. This has significantly increased the level of public engagement with the issues and shaped a distinct culture and community of dissent among the activists. Like the undocumented protestors in Italy described by Oliveri (2012: 799), the Dreamers also demonstrate "unsuspected self-organization, self-representation and alliance-building capacities."

The movement has led to the emergence of some recognizable and vocal figures in the United States, such as Jose Antonio Vargas and Erika Andiola, a high-profile activist from Arizona. Moving fluidly between mediated spaces and platforms, their narration of the high points of their lives without papers builds on the prevailing belief that the communal sharing of stories can lead to renewed and democratic participation (Lénárt-Cheng and Walker, 2011). Both Vargas and Andiola use their private stories as a pivotal focus of attention, a point of entry to talk about the commonalities in the larger shared script of the undocumented. Soon after her mother was handcuffed and taken away by immigration agents, Andiola posted a YouTube video where she makes an emotional statement about deportation and its impact on families: "We need to do something, we need to stop separating families. This is real. This is so real. This is not just happening to me, this is happening to families everywhere." The YouTube video went viral and social media activated a national response leading to the return of her mother. Andiola posted a status update on her Facebook page thanking the whole country at large: "the reality is, you made this happen! My mami is home because of your calls."[26] The appeal, which crossed spatial and virtual geographies, called out to the nation to take responsibility for the grief that breaks apart undocumented families. The deportation and dramatic media intervention have since endowed Andiola with an emblematic status and highlighted the social and transnational repercussions of deportations.

Vargas, the cause célèbre of the immigrant rights movement, has used his media presence to "come out" both as undocumented and gay, as we have seen. Soon after the *New York Times* (Vargas, 2011) article appeared, he fielded questions on an AMA (Ask Me Anything) forum on Reddit, a social networking and news website, using his life story as a point of departure for the wider discussion: "Hi, happy to be doing this chat. Thank you for joining us. As a gay, undocumented Asian guy with a Latin name – it's called Filipino – I'm like a walking uncomfortable question to some people. And I'm all for having uncomfortable, honest conversations so we can fully understand what is at stake in this immigration conversation."[27] With the weaving together of immigration, race, and sexuality, the activists articulate a political subjectivity that reflects the complex configurations and identity positions that stand outside forms of normative citizenship. The idea of "coming out" has been powerfully mobilized to activate a coalitional politics around immigration.[28] Leading lives that confront multiple and layered dimensions of power, the undocumented use performative tactics drawn from the realities of their everyday struggles. For example, in an interview Vargas mentions how those who balance multiple minoritized subject positions are forced to make impossible choices. He adds that it is comparable to being asked: "What part of you is more equal than the other?"[29] By highlighting the oppressive and entangled social formations that frame their bodies and presence in the nation, the undocumented are transforming forms of advocacy and queering the debate at the same time. The introduction of a queer politics as a resistant strategy both reveals the limits of the dominant discourse of citizenship and refuses its racial and sexual normative and authentic definitions (Gopinath, 2005; De Genova, 2010; El-Tayeb, 2011). Queering the terrain of immigration radically denaturalizes the stability and coherence of identity categories that have traditionally served as the basis for defining nationalism and citizenship.[30]

The ground of political action emerges, according to Rancière, when "certain subjects that do not count create a common polemical scene where they put into contention the objective status of what is 'given' and impose an examination and discussion of those things that were not 'visible', that were not accounted for previously" (Rancière and Panagia, 2000: 125). The players and the various examples discussed here illustrate the struggle to gain voice and visibility from locations deemed illegitimate. Defying categorization, the undocumented in various global sites are performatively exposing complex forms of exclusion and raising difficult questions about rights, status, and citizenship. Speaking in a register deemed out of place, they are asserting themselves as political actors and engaging in storytelling, media productions, public protest, and vibrant networking. The innovative use of technology and mediated activism has set into motion the choreography of assembly (Gerbaudo, 2012) and a highly charged interactive dialogue about papers, bureaucracy, sexuality, bodies and the meaning of presence and legitimacy.

# 3   Recognition:
## Politics and Technologies

> Why try to think the categories of citizenship and disaster together? The answer is that the association of citizenship with disaster and the characterization of certain populations as being more susceptible to disaster than others show that citizenship is not a stable status that one simply struggles to achieve, but an arena of conflict and negotiation.
>
> Azoulay, 2008: 31

On subways, trains, and buses, New York City commuters cannot miss the posters that caution them ominously: "If you see something, say something." These posters, which started appearing soon after September 11, 2001, appeal to citizens to get involved and collaborate with law enforcement in monitoring the city for suspicious behavior or activity. Developed by a New York advertising agency for the Metropolitan Transportation Agency (MTA) of New York and later adopted by the US Department of Homeland Security, the slogan is now used in a variety of institutional contexts and cities across the United States and has even been adopted in cities in Australia.[1] Soon after the reports of the unattended knapsack from the Madrid bombing, the MTA reworked the posters and added the words "be suspicious of anything unattended." This campaign has become a marketing success story and the public at large have incorporated this state of watchfulness into their everyday lives.

In 2010, a vendor of T-shirts in New York City reported a smoking automobile and averted a bomb from blowing up in the crowded Times Square area. The vendor and Vietnam veteran Duane Jackson's action saved the day and he became an instant hero, with tourists wanting to take pictures with him. When reporters asked for a comment about his action, he had just one phrase to share: "if you see something, say something."[2] It is true that Duane Jackson might have stopped a catastrophe in the making. However, other citizens are routinely seeing and hearing terror in accents, sounds, features, and faces of difference. In its many iterations, the slogan has succeeded in conflating vigilant seeing and timely speaking with civic duty and patriotism. How is the criterion of *something-ness* used to identify bodies and determine that they warrant being sighted and reported? What is the *something* that is being perceived and how does this information move and morph? The answers to these questions are generated by the ontologies of risk that are increasingly used to navigate the global city and its perva-sive culture of fear. Citizenship itself, as Azoulay (2008) argues, becomes a site of conflict and contestation. With constant repetition, the visual and audible cues of risk and foreignness have become part of a distributed inventory of common knowledge. The recognition of the "something" and the sense of surety about it are now amplified through the avenues of digital media. Appadurai's (2006) discussion of the uncertainties that characterize the global present are highly relevant in this context as well.

> Each kind of uncertainty gains increasing force whenever there are large-scale movements of persons (for whatever reason), when new rewards or risks attach to large-scale ethnic identities, or when existing networks of social knowledge are eroded by rumor, terror, or social movement. Where one or more of these forms of social uncertainty come into play, violence can create a macabre form of certainty and can become a brutal technique (or folk discovery-procedure) about "them" and, therefore, about "us." (Appadurai, 2006: 6)

In the process of categorizing certain individuals and groups, the bodies of immigrants become stigmatized surfaces of fear and the everyday is reconstituted as a site of uncertainty and threat. The social anxieties and political perturbations around the subject of immigration have become a recurring feature of public life in the global context. In the United States the crises over immigrant groups have played a very significant role in the reiteration of dominant versions of national identity. Over the years, the restrictions placed on immigrants have consolidated the cultural mythology of the nation by marking the distinctions between insiders and outsiders. Immigration is a classic site of biopolitics where bodies are disciplined, regulated, and managed.[3] Immigrants and refugees are objectified and managed within what Butler and Athanasiou (2013: loc. 1641) call a moral economy of obligatory vulnerability. This precarity and associated violence in immigrant lives are deeply tied to the nation's insecurities about its own changing demographic and racial composition.

These issues are particularly relevant today, when various technologies of vision are deeply entrenched within civilian spaces and increasingly mimic zones of border policing and securitization. The patriotism of citizens in a networked world are being performed in newer digitized spaces but within familiar exclusionary rhetorics. When race and biology are being rewritten today in the language of information, the body becomes both a database to be targeted and simultaneously a site of control.[4] This recent informationalization of the immigrant body gains a distributive credibility precisely because it digitally isolates the threatening racialized image of the immigrant, in contradistinction to the patriotic citizen. This figuration of the immigrant serves as a rationale for the exertion of the state's disciplinary power and also for the production of forms of public vigilantism. Due to its repetitive histories, immigration discourse is like walking into a global echo chamber of things heard and experienced before. The Irish, Italian, Chinese, the Jewish diaspora and other groups have all successively faced hostile reactions on their arrival in the United States. Although the binary division between the authentic citizen and the immigrant continues to hold steady, recent events that have taken place in the United States reveal how the politics of Othering has assumed new twists and variations in its latest digital iterations. This chapter turns to the digital rewriting of these old anxieties and how prevailing paradigms of certainty are deployed in the crowd-sourced discovery of Otherness. How are the face and racial presence of the immigrant Other recognized, refused recognition, misrecognized, and rendered intelligible?

The identification and categorization of Otherness quickly slide into a process of demonization that is rapidly facilitated by the flow of information and the circuits of social media. As governments legitimize their policies and control in the name of safeguarding against risk, the public is ready to act in ways that respond to "perceived" security threats. Risk management becomes the ground and mode of agreement between citizens and governments (Isin, 2004: 218). Today, the face of risk is the face of the brown, South Asian, or Middle Eastern immigrant; a face, construed in generalities, that conjures danger, evokes fear and images of primitive chaos and cultures of barbarism. How does this composite face, the singular face of many faces, begin to populate the national imaginary? How do we begin to map these mediations and representations whose meanings span space and time? These responses of fear, racism, and surveillance that link faces, fear, and danger have long genealogies and wide-ranging trajectories of circulation, from newspaper reports and cable news to digital discussions in social media. As suspicion is spread all around everyday life, causal connections link faces, race, and danger. Distant places and realities are combined within the frame of the local and come to bear on specific faces. Immigrant bodies are remade as surfaces of suspicion where highly visible and everyday routine forms of violence meet.

## Digital Hunt

On April 15, 2013, two pressure-cooker bombs exploded during the Boston Marathon near the finish line on Boylston Street. After the bombing, law enforcement officers began searching databases, conducting interviews, and reviewing surveillance footage from local businesses. Three days later, the Federal Bureau of Investigation (FBI) released photographs and surveillance video of two suspects who were identified later as two brothers, Dzhokhar and Tamerlan Tsarnaev. According to most reports they were identified by their aunt, who called the FBI tip line. After the photographs were released, the brothers, who were on the run, killed a police officer and carjacked a vehicle owned by a Chinese immigrant, who later called the police. In a dramatic sequence of events, Tamerlan Tsarnaev was shot by the police, then run over by the car driven by his brother Dzhokhar and pronounced dead.[5] In a manhunt that ensued in the Boston suburb of Watertown, a local resident found Dzhokhar hiding in a boat covered in blood. The entire hunt for the Tsarnaev brothers was also an intense social media event where a networked public aggressively participated in identifying suspects within the space of the digital enclosure.

Images of the Tsarnaev brothers are now part of the visual archive of this horrific event. Pictures of the two at various stages of their lives have been circulated globally. Tamerlan, the star boxer, was, according to media reports, more attached to his Muslim faith and hence less assimilated. These two facts, of Muslim faith and assimilation, are projected almost always as antithetical and standing in an impossible opposition. The photographs of the younger Dzhokhar are by now etched in public culture: Dzhokhar walking with his backpack, with his baseball cap turned backwards, his picture from his profile on VKontakte, the Russian social networking site, his high-school graduation picture. The image that gained most notoriety has been the one of Dzhokhar looking like a rock star on the cover of *Rolling Stone* with the caption: "How a popular, promising student was failed by his family, fell into radical Islam and became a monster."[6] There were no images in the magazine that would have confirmed public expectations of the angry, brown-skinned Muslim terrorist.[7] The *Rolling Stone* article projected the angle that Dzhokhar or Jahar was "a normal American kid" who liked soccer, hip-hop, and girls, obsessed over television shows like *The Walking Dead* and *Game of Thrones*, and smoked copious amounts of weed. Dzhokhar, by this account, is made out to be a regular young man, all assimilated into American life, and with no one in his social network picking up what he would or had become. As introduced by the magazine's editors, the article was intended as "a riveting and heartbreaking account."[8] The story about the un-extraordinary background of a terrorist was trending on Twitter, and incited much anger and public resistance, especially in digital forums.

In the hours and days after the bombing, there was a collective frenzy over photographs and faces and a race to identify the suspects. The violence on the streets of Boston was ghastly, and in the frenzy that followed, fingers were being pointed at possible suspects. Who was the Boston bomber? When the Boston police released surveillance video gathered from commercial establishments, they solicited the help of the public to identify the suspects. This, in turn, set off a hysteric reaction that spread quickly online and completely engrossed networked publics of social media. The intense detective work began to spread online with active discussions and commentary about possible suspects. Information was exchanged rapidly in the digital domain about likeness and resemblances. Speculations were tweeted, retweeted, and circulated to a sea of users. An unstoppable cascade of information flow was set into motion.

The stark divide between citizens and non-citizens, patriots and others, was clearly and rigidly drawn in the hours and days after the bombing. The hysteria was a continuation of the fear-mongering that has been ongoing since the events of September 11, 2001, and has taken a powerful hold on the nation. In 2001, when President Bush unveiled the list of "Most Wanted" terrorists, he announced: "Terrorism has a face, and today we expose it for the world to see."[9] In the national imaginary, there was now a prototype for the body of the outsider and for the face of the terrorist. Unfortunately, in 2013 after the Marathon bombing, the prototype merged with the face of Sunil Tripathi, a Brown University student of South Asian descent who had been missing for a month. Desperate to trace him, Sunil's family actively engaged social media and maintained a Facebook page and a Twitter account to get any current information on his whereabouts.

Crowd-sourcing to sleuthing. Image from Gawker.com *Your Guide to the Boston Marathon Bombing Amateur Internet Crowd-Sleuthing* (2013)

In a stunning sequence of events that spanned about 12 hours, the amateur detectives on social media and journalists alike were exchanging names about possible suspects and commentary about suspects. Groups like "Find Boston bomber" were quickly formed on the social networking and news website Reddit. From intent listening to the publicly available recordings of the Boston Police Department, two names started circulating with uncontrollable speed: Mike Mulugeta (the name "Mike" was never uttered on the scanner but, strangely enough, it emerged nonetheless) and Sunil Tripathi. The first tweet on this subject announced with a sense of certainty: "Suspect 1: Mike Mulugeta. Suspect 2. Sunil Tripathi."[10] This was picked up by many but notably by a journalist at Buzz Feed (an Internet news media site), who circulated the scanner information to his 81,000 followers with a follow-up message: "Wow Reddit was right about the missing Brown student per the police scanner. Suspect identified as Sunil Tripathi."[11] Excitement was clearly mounting when Luke Russert, a reporter for the US television network NBC News, tweeted a picture of Dzhokhar Tsarnaev with the message: "This pic kinda feeds Sunil Tripathi theory."[12] Driven by the downpour of hate messages, the Tripathi family took down the "Help us find Sunil Tripathi" Facebook page that they had created earlier. This action, perceived as an erasure of Tripathi's digital tracks, increased the general level of suspicion and fed into what had by now become a theory.

The removal of the Facebook page became tweet-worthy: "FYI: A Facebook group dedicated to finding Sunil Tripathi, the missing Brown student, was deleted this evening."[13] A Twitter user put out the names of two people, including Sunil Tripathi, from the Boston police scanner and in a few minutes this had been retweeted over a thousand times.[14] In a conclusive and authoritative tweet, at 3:00 am on April 19, 2013, @ YourAnonNews, the hacker collective Anonymous announced on Twitter: "Police on scanner identify the names of the Boston Marathon suspects in gunfight, Suspect 1: Mike Mulugeta. Suspect 2: Sunil Tripathi."[15] The hunt had closed in fully on Sunil Tripathi, who was missing in real life; his photographs had gained notoriety and he was found guilty and trapped in the digital hunting ground. The Internet detectives congratulated themselves that if the Tripathi theory was right, "it's changed the game 4ever."[16]

At one level, this is a story of mining the resourcefulness of the public, of empowering citizens to participate in solving security problems for the nation. It is also about the changing face of journalism and what media and communication mean in our world today. The Boston case also revealed a darker side of crowd-sourcing, where rumors and unconfirmed suspicions escalate out of all proportion. The digital domain of discussion, including Twitter and Reddit, is not always the democratic chamber of chatter, as it is often believed to be. The architecture of the platform builds in hierarchies that privilege those with a greater number of followers, with more tweet volume (Van Dijck, 2013). In the race to be fast, upvoted, and retweeted, fact and fiction blur or the distinction becomes inconsequential. In the world of Reddit, the downvote makes the story slip away from its karmic ascent.[17] As one journalist astutely put it: "The Tripathi theory had credence until it didn't and the karma balanced everything out. Unfortunately, righting things on the Internet world doesn't immediately align with reality out there in the actual world."[18] Once Sunil Tripathi was exposed, either apologies were not forthcoming[19] or the news sites rationalized the events by stating that the protocol of new media has changed the rules of the game. Participants in various discussion groups on Reddit blamed one another down the causal chain of who posted the first accusation. The brief but speedy unfurling of events revealed a great deal about the complexities of the mediated global world we live in.

Sunil Tripathi, whose body sadly washed up in a river in Providence a few days after these events, was not the only brown face to be incriminated by crowd-sourcing during the Marathon bombing. A 20-year-old Saudi national, injured while fleeing the site of the bombing, was tackled by a bystander on the spot. His apartment was raided while he was in hospital. The *New York Post* published a photograph of him with text describing him as the Saudi suspect. Images of two other young men who were carrying backpacks, the Moroccan Americans Salaheddin Barhoum and Yassine Zaime, were also scrutinized on the Internet and made the headlines in the *New York Post*: "Bag men: Feds seek these two pictured at Boston Marathon."[20] CNN's John King went on air to say that the suspect was a "dark-skinned male," [21] thereby making every non-white male a suspect. This comment drew angry criticism from several different minority groups.

Nakamura (2009: 151) makes an interesting historical observation about technology that seems pertinent to this discussion: "While early proponents of the Internet as a racially equalizing technology had stressed its ability to hide bodies or create new 'virtual' ones, after 9/11 political, technological, and cultural discourses emphasized the necessity of their radical revelation." Technology is now deployed by the state for the outing of risky bodies. This revealing of Tripathi's face cannot be explained away as the enthusiasm of a networked public, caught up in the thrill of playing digital detectives. The work of the crowd has to be situated against older and highly racialized discursive structures that fall in line with longer historical preoccupations with the hierarchies of difference. In the current climate of fear and risk, private citizens are interpellated into existing structures of surveillance as patriotic sharing subjects.[22] While the embedding of surveillance in everyday life is not new, the idea of enlisting the eyes and ears of the public has become more pervasive and has taken on a renewed importance since 2001. For example, the Tweets from the Beat program of the Boston police is fully enmeshed in the world of social media, keeping the citizenry engaged in policing practices, providing up-to-date confirmations and corrections, and appealing to the public for information.[23]

Norms about inclusion and exclusion are circulated and normalized in the realm of perception through what Rancière (2004) terms the police order, the process of distributed and mediated governance that prescribes our reality.[24] In the social media investigations and surveillance following the Boston bombing, a normalized image of the citizen was quick to surface, reiterating the very same binaries that have historically characterized the opposition to immigrants. The digital witch hunt was but the latest neoliberal and techno variant of this hostility. In his astute analysis of violence as a mediatic event, Feldman (2005: 209) notes that "as technologically structured images of catastrophe take on a life-form and agency of their own, they cease to merely report threat and become productive and reproductive mechanisms, specifying both the limits and the programmatic targets of sovereignty and governmentality." Supported by the infrastructure of technologized capitalism, a culture of consumption, and the drive for electronic entertainment, this digital version of nativism acts in concert with securitization measures adopted by the state.

## Faces, Facing, and Defacing

I next turn to the face and images of the face that played a key role in this unfolding drama. The images of Sunil Tripathi, whom his family has described in the media as "kind, gentle, shy," [25] continue to circulate and have a visible presence on the Internet, alongside those of Dzhokhar Tsarnaev. Azoulay (2012) makes a compelling argument that the encounter with the photograph continues the event of the photography that happened elsewhere. According to her, photography always constitutes a potential event; the event of photography contains within itself the potential penetrating effect of the camera. In this context, the portraits of Sunil Tripathi assumed a new visibility, from "Find Sunil" to "Wanted Sunil," and spiraled through the Internet in accelerated and disjointed encounters. Photographs from the family album, of unremarkable dailiness, assumed new meaning as they were reinserted, cropped, cut, rotated, and pasted on a path of decontextualization and resignification. "The photos bear good resemblance", writes one of the amateur sleuths on Reddit, "not perfect but there are definitely strong similarities . . . skin tone, hair color, approximate build, and yes that nose."[26] Using the visual image to arrive at various conclusions, there is, for example, discussion about hair, which is described as being tough or bushy. Finally one of the sleuths exclaims: "Whoa, I finally found a profile shot of Sunil. I would say the resemblance is pretty darn strong. Wow."[27]

With policing and surveillance processes being redefined, there is also a simultaneous construction of virtual and mediatized borders.[28] In the virtualized spaces of Reddit and Twitter, redrawn as forensic spaces, the bodies of brown men and migrants give rise to "the politics of the spectre" (Feldman, 2005: 210). The mediatized production of this investigation reworked Sunil Tripathi's face as a prototype of the wanted body. Photography as a practice itself depends on the institutions and agents that define it and set it to work (Tagg, 1993). As with all technology, the photograph is installed within specific sets of conditions. Tripathi's face in the photograph is scrutinized for specifics, even as it is depersonalized, disassembled, and criminalized. Used as a target, his body is transformed into an objectified site, intelligible only with the informational templates of other marked and profiled bodies – bodies who in the past have been mistakenly murdered, arrested, searched, and stopped for looking like, sounding like, a terrorist or having that "somethingness" that has to be reported.

For example, after the events of September 11, 2001, several South Asians of the Sikh faith were attacked, beaten, and murdered, in what was supposedly claimed to be retaliation for the attack. Frank Roque, the gunman who shot the Sikh Arizona gas station owner Balbir Singh Sodhi for looking Muslim, declared on arrest, "I stand for America."[29] As we have seen, in 2012, Wade Page, a white supremacist, opened fire, killing six people and wounding four, in a Sikh temple outside of Milwaukee in Wisconsin. Most news reports mentioned that Page might have confused Sikhs with Muslims.[30] This framing made it seem as though the shooting deaths were "less rational precisely because they rested on a misidentification" (Guterl, 2013: 44). In the Boston case, Dzhozkhar Tsarnaev turned out to be Caucasian, of Chechen origin. The interest in the Brown University student Sunil Tripathi unfolded due to his mysterious disappearance, combined with his South Asian ancestry and name. As these various stories illustrate, all brown people begin to look like terrorists in the public imaginary. The faces blend and morph into stable, identifiable types; the face mistaken remains the face not recognized. What happened in the social media groups is often explained away as the confusion or overzealous enthusiasm of young people waiting to live life like a reality show. While this may be true on some level, the "racist find Waldo,"[31] as one reporter described the events, cannot be written away as playful Internet banter. Rather the crowd sleuthing and the enactments of suspicion are embedded within longer histories of securitization and national imaginaries.

In London in 2005, as part of anti-terrorist operations, Jean Charles de Menezes, an immigrant from Brazil, was misidentified and fatally shot.[32] The Police Commissioner, Ian Blair, characterized the shooting as a tragic mistake and an unlucky accident.[33] De Menezes was mistaken for Hussein Osman, a suspect in the attempted bombings in London's transportation network, and was followed by the police when he left his own apartment. Police trailed de Menezes on the street as he contemplated taking a bus, and finally shot him seven times in Stockwell Underground Station. In an astute analysis of the case, Pugliese (2006) argues that de Menezes' walk to the station activated a regime of visuality that stereotypically transformed a Brazilian electrician into a South Asian terrorist. Pugliese notes that fantasy and fiction are transmuted into factual reality by a persistence of vision: "a racially inflected regime of visuality fundamentally inscribes the physiology of perception so that what one sees is in fact determined by the hallucinatory merging of stereotypical images" (Pugliese 2006: 3). Cautioning the US to remember the de Menezes shooting, after the publication of the two suspects in the Marathon bombing, a journalist wrote: "His only crime was to be vaguely of Islamic appearance and in the wrong place at the wrong time."[34] A religion is now securely tied to an appearance. Through a racialized reading of his skin, hair, eyebrows, gait, and clothing, de Menezes is not accidentally but systematically transmuted into an Orientalist figuration of the terrorist. To frame these events as mistakes, and to be unable to see beyond this explanation, is to be "ventriloquized," as Azoulay (2012: 9) notes, and speak in the voice of the state.[35]

Recognizability, according to Butler, is "a vexed problem," especially for those whose "only access to recognition might be through episodic media exposure or criminalization" (Willig, 2012: 140). Recognition is a constitutive part of personhood and is premised on reciprocity. In the case of immigrants, recognition is made conditional on the requirements of normative citizenship and inflected by racial dynamics. To the faces and bodies described here, there is no facework, in a Goffmanian sense, by which to legitimize one's presence. Misrecognized, there is only a face mistakenly perceived; a wrong face, and one to be ritualistically, virtually, and literally defaced.

## Cultures of Fear and Technologies of Recognition

In a systematic manner, the ordinary and the banal are co-opted into the structures of surveillance and regimes of racialized visuality. As more aspects of everyday life are brought into the realm of surveillance, the cultural and securitized production of the Other overlap. While the control of various immigrant populations has a long and highly repetitive history in the United States, the particulars of the disciplining and the related discourse are influenced and shaped by current media environments and the politics of the global present. Borders and boundaries both mark the geographies of the nation and define the composition of its national community by identifying potential citizens and classifying those who are inadmissible. Today the border apparatus itself is moving in a cellular and networked manner[36] across sites to track and discipline non-normative bodies. The border appears unannounced and unexpectedly to demarcate lives that need to be made visible as fearful objects of scrutiny, bodies that are perceived to be high risk. The economy of fear works by containing the bodies of others, a containment whose "success" relies on its failure, as it must keep open the very grounds of fear (Ahmed, 2004: 67). Part of the strategy of the border security operation is to maintain, produce, and renew a state of ongoing anxiety and a pervasive culture of fear.

These new forms of bordering practices exemplify Agamben's (1998) contention that the camp or spaces inhabited by those who have no claim on the nation are no longer confined, but generalized within the nation-state. For example, in 2011 and 2012, the Associated Press published a series of investigative articles on the New York Police Department's intelligence operations, which targeted Muslim communities, religious institutions, and other establishments owned by Muslim immigrants. According to the Associated Press, police subjected entire neighborhoods to surveillance and scrutinized where people ate, prayed, and worked, not because of any wrongdoing or accusations of crimes but because of their ethnicity.[37] In the extensive house-mapping program, the police used informants known as "mosque crawlers" to monitor sermons, and undercover officers investigated diverse sites including beauty supply stores, kebab joints, halal butcher shops, ethnic bookstores, popular hangouts, Internet cafés (to check for browsing histories of radical websites), barber shops, gyms, and taxi companies.[38] A hidden catalogue of everyday life in immigrant neighborhoods was being gathered by the state and its populations marked as part of a routine practice.

These investigative stories from the Associated Press also revealed that there was an active monitoring of immigrants who have assumed new names to blend in with the mainstream society. The surveillance methods make some commonplace immigrant activities suspect. As the Associated Press article notes: "For generations, immigrants have shed their ancestral identities and taken new, Americanized names as they found their place in the melting pot. For Muslims in New York, that rite of assimilation is now seen by the police as a possible red flag in the hunt for terrorists."[39] The blending in is no longer an assimilative gesture but a ploy to remain suspiciously hidden. The name change, a classic Ellis Island ritual and for long seen as a necessary rite of passage, is now turned around selectively, making some immigrants who Americanize their names suspect.

The politics of recognition and misrecognition also drive immigrants sometimes to construct themselves as compliant citizens. This response has to be understood against the ongoing scrutiny of Muslims in particular, and South Asian immigrants more generally, in the context of terrorism. To counter the racist and often violent politics of misrecognition after the events of September 11, 2011, some Sikh immigrants attempted to differentiate themselves from Muslim terrorists by asserting their status as model minority and dutifully loyal citizens. Some even took the opportunity to educate local communities about the peaceful nature of the Sikh religion. However, these resistant strategies, as Puar and Rai (2002: 138) argue, which are intended to make visible "Sikh commitments to American civic life," essentially legitimate "middle-class domesticity, heteronormativity, and the banal pluralism of docile patriotism."

There is a planned and ceaseless focus on immigrant bodies with the ultimate aim of creating a compendium of information that can be consolidated, cross-referenced, and linked to create complete data profiles. Automated security systems with their capacity to sort would inevitably reinforce and reproduce existing social, economic, and cultural divisions. With the possibility of monetizing risk, biometric technologies and machinic recognition systems are the hot areas of research and business today worldwide. There was a widely held belief that automated facial recognition systems might have helped avert the tragedy of the September 11 attacks. The same regret has been echoing since the attacks in Boston. Computer scientists are already writing about facial recognition systems that could have helped identify the Tsarnaev brothers given that there was a considerable amount of security video footage generated on the day of the Marathon bombings. Contrary to the popular belief that technologies are neutral conduits that can be used to solve major security concerns, Gates (2011: 101), in her astute analysis, notes that the symbolic authority of the technology in the post-9/11 context very much depended on "the idea that it could in fact be used to identify a mythic class of demonic faces that had penetrated the national territory and national imagination."

This belief in the power of technology to avert terrorism and create a compendium of risk only continues to be fortified with each new technological development. It is this same imaginary that created the digital theater where Sunil Tripathi was tried and defaced. It is this same imaginary that set off modalities of identification that travel across raced bodies, religions, and groups, collapsing cultures and politics. The misrecognition of bodies has a long genealogy in the politics of racism, slavery, colonialism, and criminology, and the roll call of names is long and keeps growing. In the year 2000 in New York City, another immigrant, Amadou Diallo, was misrecognized and fatally shot right at his doorstep. At the trial in Albany, the four white police officers were acquitted after firing 41 bullets at the unarmed 24-year -old from Guinea. The trial concluded that the shooting was an accident – "an unavoidable consequence of good police work" (Harring, 2000). The explosive question of race that clearly defined the case was never addressed. Today race is made visible and profiling justified on the grounds of national security. As these examples show, in the context of globalization, racialized affect continues to flow through the digital capillaries of power and travel rapidly through virtual geographies.

New forms of bordering practices of sovereign power, as Vaughan-Williams (2007: 187) notes, "defy conventional understandings of what and where borders are and point to the way in which alternative border imaginaries are ultimately necessary in the emerging context of the global War on Terror." Further, he makes the important argument that by reading incidents of surveillance and violence as isolated incidents or as singular erroneous acts of misrecognition, we run the risk of ignoring the broader political context in which they take place. To recognize violence as a social fact in globalization, we need to recognize violence not only in its visible, spectacular moments but also in the day-to-day reproductions of a banal nationalism, which is today fortified by what some have called a banal Orientalism (see Haldrup, Koefoed, and Simonsen, 2008). War, according to Chow (2006), is thoroughly absorbed into the fabric of our daily communications – our information channels, our entertainment media, our machinery for speech and expression. Sunil Tripathi was missing. Yet his image suffered the violence of racial profiling and subjection to "the exhaustive optics of advanced technology" (Feldman, 1994: 415). Digital media are not technologies that we merely use; nor are they just conduits in the flow of information. They become a constitutive part of the ways in which we sort the social world, recognize or misrecognize difference.

The slogan "See something, say something" is now a brand with a renewed (and unrealistic) warning to only report suspicious behaviors and situations "rather than beliefs, thoughts, ideas, expressions, associations, or speech unrelated to terrorism or other criminal activity."[40] In fact, the perceived threat posed by the faces of difference is precisely related to beliefs, thoughts, and exclusionary assumptions about the cultural coherence of the nation and its insiders. Migration is not a subject that can be understood in isolation or from the standpoint of individual migrants, but has to be situated within a complex transnational assemblage of factors where media and technology play a vital role. The narrative of migrants and migration spills and travels over complex terrain. From coffee sleeves and trains to billboards at sporting events, the slogan "See something, say something" and its culture of suspicion have become firmly ensconced in the rhythms of everyday life.

# 4 Publics:
# Eyeing Gender

Muslim women who wear the veil are not aliens.

Azmi, 2006[1]

Gender surfaces as a critical issue around which the definitions of citizenship and community are contested. Whether it is the integration of immigrants, justification for war or measuring social progress, the mediated gaze circles back to the subject of gender and sexuality. Issues get conflated when cultures and communities are represented and explained in essentialist terms. This positions cultures in opposition – those that are forward looking, and those that lack even the potential to participate in the modern present. In a sharp critique of the rigid classification of cultures, Said (2000: 581) writes that those who subscribe to this thesis see "'civilizational identity' as a stable and undisturbed thing, like a room full of furniture at the back of your house. This is extremely far from the truth not just in the Islamic world but throughout the entire surface of the globe." This classificatory scheme reproduces a worldview of modernity based firmly on the histories of European enlightenment where the West endures as the unquestioned normative center of progressive politics. This chapter examines how transnational communities contest and trouble some of these assumptions especially around the question of gender. The visual trope of the veiled Muslim woman, out of sync with modernity, has become a staple topic of media and public discourse. A stand on the veil today has turned into what Scott (2007: 17) terms an ideological "litmus test": "having an opinion about it serves to establish one's credentials on the heady topics of individualism, secularism, and the emancipation of women."

The growing presence of Muslim communities in the West has incited explosive discussions about the politics of citizenship and the integration of immigrants. Stereotypical representations of Islam reinforce perceptions of Muslims as being antithetical to the liberal subject of Western liberalism. These decontextualized conceptions quarantine Muslims in a culturalist discourse that exaggerates their Otherness and thereby legitimizes forms of exclusion. When Aishah Azmi, a 24-year-old teaching assistant in Yorkshire, England, challenged a school board's decision to suspend her because she wore the full veil, she made a powerful declaration, cited at the

53

opening of this chapter, that veiled women are not aliens. The presence of Muslim migrants in Europe is linked in the public imagination with the image of the non-assimilative Other, a politics of terror, or claims to religious visibility (Göle, 2006). The encounter with Muslim communities and their practices throws conventional multiculturalist discourses into crisis and destabilizes assumptions about the performance of citizenship. The modes of civic participation enacted by transnational migrant communities are framed as running counter to dominant frames of public life. In this climate, the subjects of immigration and gender together are a combustible combination and have evoked heated debate in various parts of Europe and the United States. How does the issue of head covering and Muslim women surface in the public domains of Western modernity? How is a Muslim woman's style of dress and head covering perceived as a viable mode of public presence and engagement? How does this impact the performative possibilities and enactments of citizenship available to Muslims, particularly veiled Muslim women in the West?

With the growth of transnationally connected communities and complex forms of national affiliation, the transparency, singularity, and nation-centered conceptualizations of the public sphere cannot be assumed. Foregrounding some of the presuppositions worked into public discourse enables a mapping of how social worlds are reproduced, regulated, and disciplined. The manner in which questions are being raised about citizenship, integration, and community has serious consequences for democratic public engagement. The tensions between dominant national narratives and transnational cultural processes heighten the contested nature of public life in contemporary Western societies. When the topic of Muslim women appears in the media, cultural differences are almost immediately cast in terms of a civilizational clash, and the gendered body of the immigrant Other surfaces either as a spectacle or as a subject to be rescued. The typical script is of the enlightened West exerting its pastoral power to save the gendered body of the immigrant from a putative, premodern, and oppressive religious structure. Right from colonial times, Muslim women have been used strategically as a rationale for the exertion of benevolent power. In particular, the dress codes of Muslim women have come to signify their subordinate status and lack of agency. The veil has been endowed with a formidable range of political and symbolic meaning, and the practice of veiling almost instantaneously marks the Muslim woman as a premodern subject, embedding her within a religious system that is portrayed as being inherently illiberal and oppressive (Ayotte and Husain, 2005; Ezekiel, 2006; Ware, 2006; Abu-Lughod, 2013). The rhetoric about veiling, which has surfaced in various registers throughout European colonial history, is currently being rescripted and deployed within the context of global migration and the security state. This chapter examines how questions of gender gain visibility and are inserted into the continuing debate about the integration of Muslim transnational communities. I discuss particular ways in which the head cover worn by Muslim women is used in public discourse to frame the debate about new publics and their public presence. The practice of veiling makes the headlines in global media with striking regularity. The debate, for example, in France and the French ban on the public wearing of the full-face veil received a great deal of global attention and controversy. Since then other countries like Belgium and some cities in Spain and Italy have brought in similar bans,[2] and these issues continue to erupt. The argument against the veil most often rests on the premise that covering inhibits face-to-face communication. Here I focus on comments made in 2006 by two British politicians about Islam and the veiling practices of Muslim women. The comments serve as a point of departure from which to elaborate on how questions of difference and religio-political issues, especially with respect to Muslim women, take center stage. Although these comments have been covered extensively in the media, the views expressed and arguments made about immigrants and integration continue to be repeated with different inflections. I elaborate on these arguments and their implications in order to draw attention to the manner in which difference is publicized and connected with the idea of a communicable gendered subject.

In late 2006, Jack Straw, a senior British politician, wrote a newspaper column about Muslim women's head covering that sparked intense discussion around the world. Writing about an interaction in his office with a covered Muslim woman, Straw confessed that he felt "uneasy talking to someone face-to-face who I could not see."[3] Around the same time, the then prime minister, Tony Blair, in a critical speech on multiculturalism admonished immigrants to adhere to the nation's "essential values."[4] The column by Straw presents the actual demand made to Muslim women to conform to performative conventions, and Blair's remarks about integration set the expectations about the imagined community of the nation. Together these two examples advance a discussion about the nature and form of publicness and its largely unquestioned universality. Warner (2002: 8) argues that there are "ambiguities, even contradictions" in the idea of the public, and notes that as it extends "to new contexts and new media, new polities and new rhetorics, its meaning can be seen to change in ways that we have scarcely begun to appreciate." Responding to this challenge, I ask what forms of publicity and public belonging mean in the transnational context when global communities are scripting new forms of public presence and comportment. What are the modalities of public engagement that are set in motion when actors with distinct cultural and political trajectories interact? How are questions of modernity and tradition inserted into the discussion on gender in terms of symbolic meaning and material effects?

## Uncovering the Alien Within

Since September 11, 2001, Muslim women's head cover, long a trope for the oppression and subordination of women, has surfaced as a prominent subject of attention. The conflation of the veil with women's passivity and primitivism both oversimplifies and flattens the Muslim experience in highly problematic ways. In October 2006, Jack Straw, the British Labour Party politician and former foreign secretary, stirred up a round of publicity for Muslim women, the Islamic dress code, and its appropriateness in British public life. In his weekly column in the *Lancashire Telegraph*, Jack Straw described a meeting where he had requested a Muslim woman, who had come to his constituency's advice bureau, to remove her veil. The woman, whom he does not name, was wearing a *niqab* or full veil, so that her face, except for her eyes, was fully covered. To Straw, this was a "visible statement of separation and of difference."[5] The article sparked national debate in Britain about identity, inclusion, and the very possibility of a multicultural society. As expected in the media-saturated environment, the comments caused international ripples, escalated debate, and drew heated reactions from around the world.

Straw maintained that he defends the right of the woman to wear a head-scarf and wearing a full veil breaks no laws. Yet he states in the column:

> The conversation would be of greater value if the lady took the covering from her face. Indeed, the value of a meeting, as opposed to a letter or phone call, is so that you can – almost literally – see what the other person means, and not just hear what they say.
>
> I thought it may be hard going when I made my request for face-to-face interviews in these circumstances. However, I can't recall a single occasion when a lady has refused to lift her veil; most seem relieved.
>
> Last Friday was a case in point. The veil came off almost as soon as I opened my mouth. I dealt with the problems the lady had brought to me. We then had an interesting debate about veil wearing. This contained some surprises. It became clear that the husband played no part in her decision. She had read books about the issue. She felt more comfortable wearing the veil when out. People bothered her less.[6]

One must pay attention to the tenor of Straw's comments and to the juxta-position of facts that he presents – "the husband played no part in her deci-sion."[7] Straw also adds earlier in the column "her husband, a professional man I vaguely knew, was with her. She did most of the talking. I got down the detail of the problem, told them that I thought I could sort it out, and we parted amicably."[8] To Straw, the fact that the husband was silent in this interaction is a very important indicator of her autonomy and agency. He goes on to say (perhaps with some surprise and condescension?) that she had read books about the issue. The very articulation of this statement reinforces the stereotypical construction of the Muslim woman as one who, through her own veiling, sets herself apart as both unthinking and premodern.

Why is Straw so ill at ease? After all, the woman who came in to his office got her work done, as he claims in the column. In his own words, the lady in question was perfectly articulate and they transacted the business she came for, and in addition, she seems to have graciously lifted her veil at his request. Straw continued to defend himself by saying the veil was "a visible statement of separation and of difference."[9] He believed it stood in the way of community relations and reinforced the creation of parallel communi-ties. Straw's admission of his discomfort comes from the belief in the revela-tory aspect of the face and its primacy in the normative Western modes of sociality. Several questions emerge: should he have made the request? Why is the veil relevant to the conduct of his duties? Why the need to see her face unveiled? What are the assumptions about the face with respect to comport-ment in public? How does Straw's role as a public official authorize and/or legitimize his request. As Williams (2006: 9) writes in the *Nation*, "when Straw insists that Muslim women who come to his office remove their veils for his comfort, who is the host and who is the guest? Is his role properly the accommodating public servant or more the gatekeeper of Anglican mores?" Muslim women's avowals of choice and assertions of comfort with the veil are most often dismissed, argues Williams (2006), as false consciousness.

Lecturing to an inter-faith gathering after the heated reaction to his column, Straw continued on the theme of assimilation: "Simply breath-ing the same air as other members of society isn't integration."[10] Many might consider these comments to be harmless statements or requests from a senior politician with an impeccable record of public service. However, the implications of the statements, and his position of privilege that gives him the authority to make them, warrant further consideration. After the speech at the inter-faith gathering, the BBC reported that a veiled woman in the audience made a comment to Straw: "I recognize that you feel uncom-fortable. I sympathize in a way but I don't accept that these women who visited your surgery are less integrated. I don't feel any less British or feel

Jack Straw canvassing, 2005 © Odd Andersen/Getty

any less common value with British society."[11] It is this space of hybrid-ity, a lived and unrecognized cosmopolitanism, and the ability to perform Britishness differently that unsettle the coherence of the normative narrative of citizenship.

## Modes of Publicizing Difference

At the heart of this debate lies the subject of Britishness and the ideological constructs embedded within what are considered core British values. The Muslim women's *niqab*, or full cover, gains center stage as an impediment to assimilation or as "a mark of separation," as Tony Blair termed it.[12] This discourse about the veil first focuses on what is essentially a woman's choice of clothing; it then moves to draw conclusions in linear sequence about larger questions of the nation, integration, and the imagined community. What is also striking about this debate is the manner in which issues of veiling, oppression, and terrorism fold into one another. This type of stereotypical slippage is becoming increasingly common, especially with the rise in anti-immigrant sentiments in the West.

Commenting on both Jack Straw's remark and Azmi's suspension for refusing to remove her veil in school, Tony Blair, the prime minister at that time, stated: "We have to deal with the debate. People want to know that the Muslim community in particular, but actually all minority communities, have got the balance right between integration and multiculturalism."[13] This characterization and framing of the debate provide a telling comment on the state of multiculturalism in Britain. Blair and Straw assert that the debate is not about choice but about effective communication. To the Muslim community in Britain, the debate is about yet another form of stigmatization that further separates them from the larger polity. Blair's comments reveal the limits of the national imaginary with respect to immigrants and the performative modalities deemed permissible for full participation in public life.

Islam is considered the fastest-growing religion in Europe and the presence of Muslim immigrants acts as a flash point triggering discussions about religion, cultural integration, and citizenship. The aggressive blaming of immigrants and the call for certain types of integration reveal the increasing levels of national anxiety about the presence of Others and the perception of the passing away of a familiar, homogenous public. In the process of excluding Muslim presence from the public whole, a long and complex history of transnational connections between Islam and the West is forgotten and erased. In addition, the political conversation about immigration and diversity is substituted for a cultural and civilizational discourse, a change that ultimately oversimplifies and aggravates the situation. As Göle (2006: 14) writes, "Europeanness appears as an identity defined by shared history and common cultural values rather than as a project for rethinking the political bond."

It is the evocation of intangible abstractions that serves as the fault line for separating the truly integrated from the so-called resistant immigrants. In his 2006 speech on multiculturalism, Tony Blair provided a series of declarations stating that immigrants should subscribe to the essential values that give citizens the right to be called British. Blair's comments set the tone for the larger political climate in which the earlier discussion about Straw has to be situated. "Integration . . . is not about culture or lifestyle. It is about values. It is about integrating at the point of shared, common, unifying British values. It isn't about what defines us as people, but as citizens, the rights and duties that go with being a member of our society."[14] In an appeal to a lost homogeneity through these generalizations, any critical discussion on the shared politics of multiculturalism is circumvented. Instead the rhetoric points solely to immigrants as the implosion from within, as this comment from Tony Blair indicates: "But how do we react when that 'difference' leads to separation and alienation from the values that define what we hold in common?"[15]

This warning about liberal multiculturalism arises from an underlying antipathy to immigrants that is fortified by the argument regarding cultural incompatibility. There is also an aggressive stance that confounds the very logic of tolerance and acceptance that Blair propounds: "Our tolerance is what makes Britain, Britain. So conform to it; or don't come here."[16] The call to conform and Blair's insistence that immigrants have a "duty" to integrate were interpreted by many to mean that Britain's multiculturalist experiment was over. Blair's remarks, which were echoed widely in media reports, reflect British society's dominant attitude toward difference and the scrutiny directed at Muslim citizens. It reveals the anachronism of operating under a fixed notion of a homogenous public sphere. What we see happening here is the recuperation of a national ideology that resists the very idea of difference as a basis for building community. At the same time, the presence of deterritorialized cultures and transnational communities destabilizes inflexible assumptions about boundaries and singular forms of national allegiance. Blair unequivocally upholds the transcendence of a singular national community that subsumes and erases the particularities of all other counter-publics:

> But when it comes to our essential values – belief in democracy, the rule of law, tolerance, equal treatment for all, respect for this country and its shared heritage – then that is where we come together, it is what we hold in common; it is what gives us the right to call ourselves British. At that point, no distinctive culture or religion supersedes our duty to be part of an integrated United Kingdom.[17]

Blair's injunction overlooks the complexities of everyday life within transnational communities. The maintenance of webs of diasporic affiliations that exceed national borders and the production of new forms of translocal cultures both threaten and produce a crisis in the Western imaginary.[18] The debate about who's in and who's out is rehearsed everywhere from schools and hospitals to airport security. Categories such as here and there, West and East, are, and have always been, deeply implicated in one another. As people cross borders, cultures are reinvented and mix on the street, but the language of assimilation and obligation to the mythos of national community ironically remains strong and clear.

In the context of globalization and increased security, it is revealing to pay attention to the processes and modalities through which publics are actualized (Brouwer and Asen, 2010). The public sphere, in its ideal Habermasian form, is considered an arena where the rational discourse and deliberation of citizens can influence public policy and the generation of public opinion. However, in the case discussed here we see both an active steering of the nature of public debate about immigration and a specification of the terms under which a national public is constituted. Various regimes of cultural normativity are cited to structure the ways in which private citizens should be inducted into fields of publicity as rightful citizens. Blair's comments, cited in this discussion, demonstrate how notions of the public and public good are shaped and mobilized within fields of power. The debate is significant as it involves the demarcation of national boundaries and the valorization of a singularly defined national public.

In spite of cultures becoming increasingly deterritorialized and transnationalized in everyday practices, the conception of the public and the public sphere also remains deeply entrenched within nationalist presuppositions (Fraser, 2005). Immigration provides a good example of the fact that the state and the public sphere are not as distinct or separate as in the original Habermasian formulation (Asen and Brouwer, 2001). The state is closely involved in the constitution and surveillance of the public through the demarcation of boundaries to identify both national spaces and rightful citizens. Ironically in the global context, economic policies are striving to create border-free spaces for the free circulation of capital and commodities, while immigration policies remain rooted within older conceptions of the bounded nation-state and national borders (Sassen, 1999).

The immigrant wearing visible symbols of religion becomes the ultimate marker of difference in a national space that continues to consider itself cosmopolitan, tolerant, and anti-racist or even post-racial. On a self-congratulatory note, Blair extols this space:

> Our public culture is also completely different. We now have more ethnic minority MPs, peers, and Ministers though not enough. We have had the first black Cabinet minister. The media are generally more sensitive, and include ethnic minority reporters and columnists. Racism has, for the most part, been kicked out of sport. Offensive remarks and stupid stereotypes have been driven out of public conversation. The basic courtesies, in other words, have been extended to all people.[19]

Blair's view of a culture of tolerance uniting the country summons a social landscape that is totally disconnected both from the complexities of the imperial past and from the contested terrain of contemporary life. Deepseated antagonisms cannot be unsettled so easily. Selectively recognizing public culture in terms of a superficial multiculturalism, Blair claims a national victory over racism. For both Blair and Straw, the idea of the public is deeply entrenched within the ideological framework of a dominant discourse of citizenship. Racial and gendered modalities of casting difference are worked deeply into the assumptions that drive the machinery of nationalism. In the last quote from his speech, Blair claims stupid stereotypes have been driven out and basic courtesies have been extended to all people. Through such rhetorical fiats, racism is presented first and foremost as an individual and behavioral lack rather than as a systemic politics of exclusion.

Nationalism and a fervent call for re-homogenization become the primary response to the fear that the arrival of immigrants has caused the demise of cohesion and social harmony. The reality of colonialism and the contested relationship between transnational and national cultures are erased from the discussion in a drive to sanitize the public sphere. The focus on immigrants should be viewed, as Gilroy (2004: 149) argues, as part of Europe's history rather than its contemporary geography. By assigning the immigrant "problem" to the immediate present, the politics and histories of difference are elided and solutions are posed as strategies for assimilation. The nationalist narrative premised on the hegemony of Western modernity is enforced through the stipulation of a series of exclusions. According to Gilroy (2004: 150), "when migrancy supplies the decisive element, the door gets opened to patterns of explanation that ultimately present immigrants as authors of their own misfortune. The violence and hostility regularly directed at them by their reluctant hosts can then be excused."

In the next section I return to Jack Straw's comments in order to discuss the conditions of possibility that are presented to the gendered transnational subject in the context of this beleaguered multiculturalism.


## Staging of the Modern Citizen

Citizenship is associated with some very real material and performative expectations that are evoked by Straw and others. The long, colonial history behind the Western gaze directed at Islam has received a new Orientalist twist conflating Islam, irrationality, fundamentalism, violence, gendered oppression, and terrorism (Ahmed, 1993; Scott, 2007). The veiled woman becomes the focus of attention, and prejudices about the Muslim world are channeled through a discourse of benevolence and righteousness. The political justification of the US-driven war on terror as one intended to liberate women, Laura Bush's cry of outrage about the oppression of her Afghan sisters,[20] and these remarks by Straw and Blair all follow suit in their easy assignment of victim status to Muslim women. As Najmabadi (2006: 244) asks, how has the veil become "the almost exclusive visual sign of radical cultural difference between Islam and Europe?" The refrain around the veil has been consistent – Muslim women have no agency and need to be liberated by Western enlightenment. The veil sets off a series of doubts and questions about not only gender oppression in the Islamic community and the ability of Muslim women to act independently but also the very possibility of Muslim women partaking of modernity. The veil radically unsettles the private/public distinctions of the secular liberal paradigm complicating the terms of intelligibility within public culture.[21]

The perception of Muslim women as a threat to secular democracy provides a striking illustration of the rigidity and the privileged religio-political referents worked into the constitution of the public sphere. Straw's request that women abandon the veil to facilitate conversation is fraught with assumptions that lay out the terrain against which difference is measured and regulated. With no swerving from the register of polite benevolence, the expectations and regulations are mobilized to secure the national space. Let us return to a few of Jack Straw's assertions where he notes inconsistencies between the attire of the woman who was in his office and her performative stance. Straw notes that the woman spoke in a broad Lancashire accent and that she was with her husband, "a professional man I vaguely knew," but "she did most of the talking."[22] After acknowledging that the particular encounter was polite and respectful on both sides, Straw writes it got him thinking: "In part, this was because of the apparent incongruity between the signals which indicate common bonds – the entirely English accent, the couple's education (wholly in the UK) – and the fact of the veil."[23] Her visual presentation and material presence wearing a *niqab* call into question the authenticity of her Britishness and her performance of citizenship. This exchange cannot be dismissed as a request from a seasoned politician about the inability to make contact with the full face of a member of his constituency. It speaks to the contested politics of global migration, multiculturalism, and the assumptions that underwrite the national community.

Straw's comment emanates from the liberal premise of the speaking subject and a particular type of visual representation. To Jack Straw, the woman (who is never named or identified), her persona, and her public performance were misaligned with the present and the modern. Her embodied presence, characterized by Straw as "a visible statement of . . . difference,"[24] defied a certain type of required transparency. On account of her covered appearance, she is, in turn, denied admittance into the community of citizens. The *niqab* does not allow the woman, in Straw's interpretation, to participate in modernity as she lacks the appropriate look, and hence she and other Muslim women are actively setting themselves apart in "voluntary apartheid," as another British politician termed it.[25] Straw pays no attention to the complex colonial and racist overtones of his own so-called request. Saving women, as mentioned earlier, has been a central trope in the legitimizing of the colonial project and continues to be so in the current geopolitical context. Straw repeats the same formulaic Western response to veiled Muslim woman by reducing the veil to a visible sign of disempowerment and collapsing the diversity of the Muslim experience into a singular and reductive explanation centered on the veil (Abu-Lughod, 2002, 2013). Using the rhetoric of neoliberalism, Straw also couches the issue as one of personal choice by suggesting that someone with a Western education should know better. What Straw seems to be asking is how someone with a British education and upbringing could be so regressive as to accept a veil as a form of attire. Not only does Straw simplify the cultural practice of veiling but he links it to the question of his comfort in communication: "Above all, . . . I felt uncomfortable about talking to someone 'face-to-face' who I could not see . . . It was such a visible statement of separation and of difference."[26]

Ultimately it is Straw's discomfiture that triggered the "request" to remove the veil, as well as the immediate global media attention that followed about the ability of Muslim women to integrate, and the expected anti-Muslim reaction. As a white male politician, Jack Straw could pay attention to his interpersonal discomfort and circumvent the power differential embedded in the encounter. He bypasses the fact that he is able to make this "request" from his position of privilege as a white male politician. In her column in the *Guardian*, Bunting (2006) argued "comfort is a disastrous new measure for interactions in a diverse society." In his concern for Britishness, Straw's comments led to more intense anti-Islam reactions and in fact fortified the politics of parallel communities. The veil becomes the target through which to isolate Muslim women and cast them as stigmatized figures not belonging to the modern.

The narrative of modernity, especially in the case presented here, has been constructed with Europe at the center in terms of both its geographical location and temporal flow. The linear path of progress against which other cultures are measured and regulated is normed on the West. With the universalism of the project established, modernity reproduces itself through "assigning a different and lesser significance to things deemed purely local, non-Western and lacking a universal expression" (Mitchell 2000: xi). What is incompatible with the so-called modern is rendered marginal or deficient, only to be measured as a lack or an aberration. In the essentialized discourse about culture that is widely circulated today, cultures are distinguished in simplistic terms or described as innate and static qualities that inhere in groups of people. The culture talk we hear today splits the world, according to Mamdani (2005), into the modern on the one hand and on the other the premodern, who are either lagging behind on the road to modernity or else are decidedly anti-modern.

Chakrabarty (2000) advances a compelling argument that modernity is always depicted as a transition narrative for the non-West and a narrative about a lack. The West stands in as the end point, the destination for the rest of the world, which is forever delegated to the "waiting rooms of history," lacking coevalness and contemporaneity with the West. The veiled woman, by extension, exists in an ahistorical framework; her status reified as out of step with modernity and its rational expectations. In a re-narration of a colonial gesture, Straw's remarks stand in for the imperial center offering its benevolence to help the Muslim woman step across the threshold, the operative assumption being that rescuing the gendered subject from her cultural confines will deliver her into the present and a communicable modernity. Straw, in fact, wants to assist in the birth of the modern gendered Muslim subject.

Postcolonial scholars theorize that modernity and its institutions should be linked to the colonial modes of knowledge production and structures of power rather than be viewed as merely a European invention or a time period through which all societies must pass. The space of colonial difference has always been a pre-condition for the staging of the modern with the subaltern subject defined as the constitutive Other of modernity. In order to perform its authority, modernity must distinguish itself aggressively from what it conceives of as the non-modern. To do so, it defines its rationality and enlightenment in opposition to traditionalism and the irrationality of Others. This tension is framed as the divide that stipulates how and which forms and modalities of Otherness can be accommodated within the space of the West.

## Conclusion

It is impossible to think of community in today's context in terms of purity or define nationalism without factoring in the realities of global migration. The insistence on homogeneity is untenable and even anachronistic in the current global context. With the increased flow of migrants from the postcolonial world into the old imperial centers, the public sphere is changing radically in terms of its composition, its form, and even its function. There is a disconnect between the state's call for assimilation to a set of core national values and the materiality of quotidian practices in transnational communities. The veil has received an inordinate amount of attention in the West. Politicians, like the ones discussed in this chapter, seem to never tire of the subject of immigrant women. Blair in his speech even apologizes for this attention but returns right back to the topic by saying "I know it is not sensible to conduct this debate as if the only issue is the very hot and sensitive one of the veil . . . it really is a matter of plain common sense that when it is an essential part of someone's work to communicate directly with people, being able to see their face is important."[27] By this evocation of common sense, the veiled subject is rendered outside of the realm of the rational. The woman in Blackburn who came to Jack Straw's office seeking assistance was transformed in the discourse that followed into a generic body out of place and spectacularly a misfit for modern forms of social interaction. The veiled woman is publicized as the one who refuses integration with the national community by not complying with obvious, commonsensical expectations of social interaction. The responsibility to adapt is placed squarely on the individual. Instead of living up to a professed multicultural vision, these speeches and injunctions to Muslim women only serve to exacerbate the tensions between communities and reproduce the rhetoric of civilizational differences. The gaze devalues the veiled Muslim woman's social presence and compromises her political agency by fixing her in terms of Otherness.

From their position of power, status, and white privilege, Jack Straw and Tony Blair stage this unveiling as an elaborate liberation or coming-out ritual for Muslim women. In fact, the focus on face-to-face communication ironically displaces any meaningful engagement about the politics of integration and multiculturalism. Gender becomes a focal point in these strategic, minoritizing maneuvers that are actively directed toward the Muslim community in Europe. The stereotypical association of a veiled woman as passive victim is linked by default to discussions about the assimilability of Muslims in Western societies. The veiled Muslim woman is brought into public view only through the benevolence of the patriarchal gaze. As Scott (2002: 9) writes, "this creates a hierarchy that promotes and reinforces a sense not just of Western superiority, but of Western women's superiority – the old colonial relationship emerges intact, an operation of domination in the guise of a mission of salvation."

Regulatory systems of exclusion that are both racialized and gendered are deeply embedded in the circuitry of nationalism and citizenship. According to Moallem (2005: 62), the imagining of an abstract citizenry rests on the construction of a civic body that sustains the authority and power of the nation-state. She argues that the civic body, in turn, rests on a logic of identity that eliminates uncertainty by eliminating Otherness. In this case, Straw's and Blair's comments suspend the Muslim woman as an exhibit on display, on the one hand making her hypervisible and on the other hand erasing her agency and particularity. The veil attaches the Muslim woman to her Otherness and disqualifies her from being part of the civic body capable of performing the scripts of normative citizenship.

The statements about the veil resurrect "fictitious unities" (Scott 2002: 9)[28] about cultural differences by mapping coherent systems of meaning to cultural groups. The consequences of this in a global environment are critical, as they reproduce the exclusionary logics on which the civic body is constructed. The unnamed women in Straw's surgery claimed her right to be a British citizen (which she was!) and at the same time exercise her freedom to express her religious affiliation and belief through the choice of her mode of dress. Here she was being a responsible, active citizen, exercising her civic identity and taking her problems to her elected representative. The only problem seems to be her choice of attire; the one that caused the alleged discomfort expressed by Straw. The veiled citizen opens up a space of contradiction that poses a radical challenge to the conventional boundaries of private and public. Interestingly enough, in spite of such comments and protest about covering, the popularity of *hijabs* with younger Muslim women has been increasing. Various forms of head scarves and coverings have gained unprecedented popularity in the West especially among young Muslim women (see Tarlo, 2010). The point is not whether this surge is a response to Straw's comments as the media would like us to believe. The significant fact is that women are choosing to veil, refuting the easy formulaic equation of veiling with oppression and acquiescence to patriarchal oppression. The use of the head cover is part of the performative expression of Muslim identity and in this context can be read as an active choice of an alternative modality of public presentation. As Macdonald (2006: 19) writes: "Expressions of surprise, even in the twenty-first century, that veiled Muslim women can appear as Olympic athletes, suicide bombers, feminist politicians, musicians or even comedians, underline the tenacity of beliefs that Islamic veiling is intrinsically incompatible with women's agency in the construction of their identities."

Veiling inserts an aspect of private identity into the public sphere and problematizes the neutrality of the secular public sphere. Muslim women in the West when they decide to follow an Islamic dress code are performing forms of embodied citizenship that test the limits of liberal discourses of freedom.[29] It identifies another set of conditions under which the gendered transnational subject will be accepted as a legitimate actor in the public domain. Other forms of head cover or even types of religious attire used by men have not drawn the same level of scrutiny as the Muslim women's head cover (see Armstrong, 2006). The woman in Straw's office is exercising her rights as a citizen but is scrutinized and criticized on the grounds of open communication. In this case, the woman's veil defies the scopic penetration of the state as symbolized by Straw's gaze and reverses the norms of visual symmetry, where the powerful male gaze has full access to the body of the subaltern. By repositioning the access to her face, the veiled woman unsettles the sensory balance of Western modernity and its public privileging of the ocular.

Straw ends his column in the *Lancashire Telegraph* with a question: "I thought a lot before raising this matter and still more before writing this. But if not me, who?"[30] Jack Straw is certainly not the only one who is raising questions about the veil today. The case discussed in this chapter reveals the limitations of using naturalized notions of difference and draws attention to the pressing need to engage with new modalities of public participation that accompany the transnational dynamics of contemporary life. In a follow-up interview, Jack Straw mentioned that "communities are bound together partly by informal chance relations between strangers – people being able to acknowledge each other in the street or being able to pass the time of day . . . That's made more difficult if people are wearing a veil. That's just a fact of life."[31] Communities are held together by history, politics, and shared experiences and not merely by chance encounters. Communication is neither transparent nor direct in the complex modalities through which publics come to be.

# 5    Domesticity:
## Digital Visions and Versions

What else do they have but the taste of those familiar dishes, which my mother can, for the most part, re-create from ingredients at the nearby A&P.
Lee, 2010: 69

Recreating the foods of one's past is as much about connecting to another place as it is about savoring flavors. In a poignant essay about the culture of food in an immigrant family, Lee (2010) recalls his mother's dismay on not finding the right ingredients in the local supermarket to make her familiar foods. "But she makes do; there's always garlic, often ginger and scallions, and passable hot peppers" (Lee, 2010: 70). This improvisation – a necessary part of a migrant's survival kit – is now enabled, prompted, and shaped by mediated possibilities.

Evoking the aromas of Indian cooking, food blogs written by South Asian diasporic women indulge their readers with culinary tales and techniques. The blogs that have gained considerable visibility present the pleasures of traditional cooking from the homeland through multimodal interweaving of text, video, links, and images. Blending details about recipes with personal anecdotes, the bloggers seem determined to secure a digital presence for themselves and give Indian food, parsed regionally, a new global visibility. While these blogs circulate specific types of culinary knowledge in a mediated global space, they also provide a space for building transnational lines of connection and reimagining diasporic identities.

Culinary secrets and family recipes, now reworked for transnational consumption, are shared with a growing networked public (boyd, 2011). These food blogs serve as a storehouse of information about the preparation of Indian delicacies and offer streamlined versions of traditional procedures suitable for the demands of global living. The reminiscences about home, homeland, and the comfort of home-cooked meals emerge within a circulatory matrix[1] where new forms of consumption and configurations of cosmopolitan sociality are being constituted. In the intimacies of the virtual kitchen, the bloggers recapture distant locales through food, actively mediate connections between tradition and modernity, and negotiate new and remembered milieus. In the process, they establish rhizomatic connections with others in the diaspora and beyond, thereby disrupting older

69

notions of diasporic alienation and insularity. Diasporic women use blogs as private memory objects (van Djick, 2007) and form a digital repository of regional flavors that leverage local origins in order to forge new transnational culinary publics.

Through the publishing of private versions and visions of domesticity, the blogs fulfill the meticulous work of cultural reproduction that has always been highly gendered in most diasporic contexts, and in particular within the South Asian community (Hegde, 1998). These "mediated microworlds" (Thompson, 1995: 233), held together by common affective ties to Indian food, reflect the continuation of feminized spaces of food preparation. The blogs enable the diasporic authors to establish intimate social networks and "different forms of dwelling, not necessarily circumscribed by geographical parameters" (Mannur, 2013: 589). The blogging templates offer a highly stylized form of self-representation along with the connective possibilities offered by nested applications and platforms. Theorizing about blogs, Dean (2010: 2) argues that contemporary communication media capture their users in intensive and extensive networks of production, enjoyment, and surveillance. While the bloggers talk about a diasporic community evolving organically from the practice of posting, commenting, and sharing, these publics are, in fact, both strategically steered by the blogging templates and defined through algorithmic calculations.

The blogs contribute to a shift in the manner and form in which Indian food circulates globally. At the moment when Indian food is trying to secure its identity and place as global haute cuisine in the West, the diasporic bloggers are claiming a cosmopolitan status for home-cooked Indian food. Through their virtual kitchens, the bloggers strive to introduce a more differentiated picture of regional Indian food. The food practices described in the blogs capture the complex levels and also new kinds of self-conscious connections that are forged between various locales (Ray and Srinivas, 2012). Culinary knowledge from the homeland via the voices and expertise of family and friends is routinely incorporated to establish standards of cultural authenticity. By creating a dynamic and ongoing dialogic bridge to India, the bloggers reshuffle the ways in which the nation, its diaspora, and globality intersect in the neoliberal context.

The composition and content of the blogs seem to stand out as a digital oasis for ruminations about home-cooked food. However, the cultural work of the blogs is situated within a broader global narrative that connects nations, foods, and changing diasporic formations. In this instance, the blogs index a particular moment and articulation of South Asian diasporic mobility that coincides with the visibility of India and Indians in the global digital economy. The mediated world of the bloggers is related to recent flows of economic migrants from India and arguably in some instances, as I will show in this chapter, to the exclusionary limits of immigration policies that prohibit dependents of skilled migrants (most of whom are men) from participating in various domains of public life (Parker, 2013). The bloggers, many of whom self-identify in the blogs as computer professionals, have all lived in and emigrated from India post-liberalization. Relocated in the West, these tech-savvy women now negotiate their minoritized locations through digital evocations of home and food. While there appears to be a sense of gendered community among these diasporic bloggers, a strong neoliberal ethos of individualism pervades the digital environment of food blogs in general. Overall, blogging provides an opportunity to turn food into a social project through the practice of authoring and negotiating the circulation of the text.

Provincializing digital media, Coleman (2010: 489) argues, will allow for "a consideration of the ways these media have become central to the articulation of cherished beliefs, ritual practices, and modes of being in the world." In this chapter, I map how South Asian women use food blogs to emplace themselves in the circuits of global modernity. I interviewed the authors of 13 popular blogs and examined their blogs carefully as an evolving visual and textual archive about Indian food and the diasporic everyday experience. The blogs signify a new moment in the transnationalization of Indian regional food, rendered possible through the home labor of diasporic women building culinary linkages to the nation. As interactive spaces anchored to the materiality of diasporic locations, food blogs written by South Asian women build networks of sociality and constitute transnational culinary publics.

## Techno Publics and Affect

As discussed in earlier chapters, communication technologies and synchronous transnational participation in everyday life have radically altered the diasporic experience (Brinkerhoff, 2009; Madianou and Miller, 2012). For these bloggers described here, unlike earlier migrants, home is always accessible via the screen, as both a resource and a support. The blogs serve as a platform for recipes, reflections, and networking. As archetypal sites of media convergence, the blogs enable the inclusion of videos, Twitter feeds, photographs, and links and blogrolls. With the cross-referencing and the flow of content between and across media, blogs open into an ever-expanding social universe along niche interests. A personalized form of social exchange, marked by collaborative rituals of turn-taking, has become customary on this digital proscenium stage. The social networking that emanates from the blog leads to the contrived formation of a "community of sentiment, a group that begins to imagine and feel things together" (Appadurai, 1996: 8). With the South Asian bloggers, the exchanges and linking occur around Indian food and its transformations.

Blogs, according to Lovink (2007: xxii), are the proxy of our time – "a techno-affect that cannot be reduced to the character of the individual blogger." While personal reflections remain the centerpiece of most food blogs, it is mainly the strategic use of links and other functionalities that draws in the readership or followers. Many view blogs as digital journals, extensions of self-representational writing characterized by reflexive, diachronic accounts of self (Serfaty, 2004). Diasporic food blogs could be seen as reworking epistolary forms of writing that have always sustained immigrant connections to lost homes (see Naficy, 2007: xiv). Using a diaristic tone embellished with the designed flow of text and visual display, the blogs strategically invite readers to engage with the site. While the blogs seem to reach out mainly to readers within the diaspora, the bloggers are clearly mindful of how and when their work is recognized by the larger food-blogging community. Some scholars emphasize that it is not useful to talk about blogs in terms of writing alone (Rettberg, 2008) or in terms of genre, like journaling (boyd, 2006). As Dean (2010: 48) notes, the focus on content alone fails to look at the practice of blogging and does not keep intersecting modes of communication in view. In the case of these blogs, solely focusing on authorial style or genre will elide the material politics of diasporic life. Hence my objective is to show how diasporic women use digital media forms to inhabit a culinary space as transient participants in a common public (Warner, 2002: 8) organized around the sociocultural world of food.[2]

The desire to blog hinges precisely on the possibilities enabled by an individually branded space and the pleasures of recognition by an expansive digital audience. The ongoing circulation of the blog text and its recursive journey through a carefully chalked map of posts, responses, rolls, and hyperlinked space set the conditions for the creation of networks and the sharing that bloggers routinely celebrate. However, it is important to note that sharing in this digital space is synonymous with drawing in traffic to one's page. If, as Lovink (2007) argues, blogging is a process of massification, then how do these shifts in scale redraw the borders between communities? In this case, are there borders that separate the diaspora from its digital neighbors?

The particularities of cultural context and the nature of transnational publics that emerge in the blogosphere merit close examination (Russell and Echchaibi, 2009). Recently research attention has focused on various global diasporic contexts where issues of digital media, everyday life, and transnational forms of affiliation intersect (Panagakos and Horst, 2006; Sreberny and Khiabany, 2010). Due to the proliferation of open-source blogging websites, setting up a blog requires no specialized technical skills. Despite the uniformity of preset templates, the diasporic food blogs are, by and large, well customized and maintained.[3] As one of the food bloggers told me during an interview, her blog site is always tidy and uncluttered like her kitchen. The well-designed virtual spaces are indeed treated like kitchens ready for the unexpected visitor. Through tales of spices and cultural narratives of food, the blogs connect localities in the West to ones in India.

## Digital Domesticity and Diaspora

South Asian women entered the world of blogging in the early 2000s, but the spurt in numbers seems to have occurred in 2005, around the same time that several blogging platforms were launched (Lovink, 2007). The food blogs have creative names such as Panfusine, Holy Cow, Indian Food Rocks, and Collaborative Curry. Most of the blogs on Indian food are written by women of the diaspora living mainly in the United States but also in other parts of the world including the UK, Canada, and UAE. While food blogs in general showcase a feminized world of domesticity, these diasporic bloggers speak to their transnationally mobile forms of belonging, in registers that are at once nostalgic, traditional, cosmopolitan, and at times postfeminist, as will be discussed later. The blogs represent a historical moment, in both the textualization and the circulation of Indian food, in terms of its global travels, identity, and connections to a more flexibly defined, diasporic experience.

The economic and cultural potential of the Indian diaspora is very influential in the social life of the nation. Koshy (2008: 33) argues that the non-resident Indian offers "a crucial vehicle for reconstructing a globalized Indian identity," especially for the rising middle class, who associate diasporic Indians with affluence and cosmopolitan cachet. The growing number of food blogs written by non-resident Indians has caught the attention of the Indian media. For example, an illustration in a national English-language daily represents the diasporic blogger in her modern kitchen wearing Western clothes and wafting the aroma of Indian food across continents (Challapalli, 2006).

The bloggers, in turn, assume an ambassadorial role with regard to Indian cuisine and react sharply to stereotypical representations of Indian food as laborious, spicy, and strange. They echo "the crusade against curry" (Roy,

2010: 159) carried out by earlier cookbook writers who sharply critiqued the continued presence of curry powder in the West. Curry, the reductive moniker – "a king of misnomers" (Banerji, 2007: 38) – has raised the ire of Indian chefs who have described it "as degrading to India's great cuisine as the term '*chop suey*' was to China's" (Jaffrey, 1975: 5). Concocted for the Victorian kitchen (Narayan, 1997; Zlotnick, 1996), this all-in-one powder continues to stand in for the diversity of India's cuisine. The bloggers renew the mission to rectify these misconceptions by speaking back to the Orientalist representations of Indian food.[4] Armed with local knowledge, they introduce regional home cooking made accessible for the cosmopolitan palate and lifestyle. While on the one hand the blogs claim to present authentic home-style cooking, they also carefully establish the malleability and adaptability of the cuisine to fit with global lifestyles. This nexus of regional and global, the leitmotif of the blogs, extends the earlier dialectic of regional and national that framed the circulatory cultures of Indian cuisine.

In an elegant exposition of the construction of a national cuisine in postcolonial India, Appadurai (1988) discusses how the twin developments of regional and national logics framed the discourse of Indian cookbooks that catered to urban cosmopolitan tastes. He argues that since the 1960s, the spread of print media, the steady rise of the middle class, and the diversification of consumption patterns have fueled the emergence and popularity of English-language cookbooks in India. With regard to the specialized, regional cookbooks, Appadurai (1988: 16) writes that they represent "a kind of 'ethnoethnicity', rooted in the details of regional recipes, but creating a set of generalized gastroethnic images of Bengalis, Tamils, Kannadikas and so forth." Building on this same tradition, the food bloggers enact their sense of national belonging through the articulation of a regional gastronomic identity. A sense of Indianness arises, as Appadurai (1988: 16) notes, "because of, rather than despite" the focus on the regional.

Food has played an important sensory role in the bonding of diasporic communities and continues to serve as a place-making practice (Ray, 2004). Cookbooks written by authors living outside of India typically evoke themes of nostalgia and memory of the homeland. It was recipes from the same cookbooks of the 1960s and 1970s, described by Appadurai (1988), that were used by immigrant women who arrived in the late 1960s in the United States, when the Hart-Celler Act opened the doors very selectively to skilled professionals and students from Asia (Leonard, 1997). In addition to the bloggers, I also interviewed six South Asian women, who emigrated between the late 1960s and 1970s when long-distance communication with India was neither affordable nor fast. They used to exchange information with other immigrant women to learn how best to incorporate ingredients like pancake mix, cottage cheese, cream of wheat, or ricotta cheese into Indian recipes. Some recall homemade folders with recipes that would arrive by mail from India. The immigration narratives of the food bloggers, however, emerge from a different migratory flow – one more recent and closely connected with India, the flows of globalization, and a more mobile sense of identity.

Since the 1990s, a large pool of Indian workers have come to the United States on temporary non-immigrant visas (H1-B visas) sponsored by specific employers, to fulfill job demands in the information technology sector. While balancing their status as members of a malleable workforce for the global economy, these new migrants also remain tightly connected to a globalized India through communication technologies, unlike their earlier counterparts (Mallapragada, 2006; Gajjala and Gajjala, 2008; Mitra, 2008). The diasporic experience of the food bloggers is unfolding at a time when the South Asian presence in the West has been well established by previous waves of migration, and ethnic spaces, Little Indias, exist in most major cities in North America. With the growing popularity of Indian food, the restaurant industry is actively refashioning an identity for Indian cuisine as global haute cuisine. Discussing the shifts in the global Indian restaurant industry, Buettner (2008: 897) notes that there has been a recent trend for restaurants to move away from clichéd names like Taj Mahal or Passage to India and instead choose names such as Cumin, Tamarind, or Cinnamon Club to demonstrate their "knowledge of sophisticated gastronomy." The cultural work of the food blogs is both enabled and sustained by these shifting patterns of South Asian mobility and the global visibility of Indian food.

## Cosmopolitics of Flexible Taste

"They are mushrooming," "there's a new one every time I look": this is how some of the bloggers describe the spurt in the number of blogs on Indian food. While it is difficult to gauge the number of diasporic food blogs, they clearly have a visible presence in blog aggregators. One blogger has launched an aggregator of popular diasporic blogs that lists close to 200.[5] I wandered into this world of blogs when faced with my own culinary dilemmas. In the liquid virtual worlds bloggers inhabit, this type of serendipitous discovery is indeed the very model of interaction that bloggers thrive on. Guided by blogrolls and hyperlinks that connect a dense world of recipes, I read the blogs closely, and then interviewed these very popular bloggers on the phone or via Skype. All the bloggers that I interviewed grew up in India and had emigrated within the previous 15 years. Seven identified themselves as information technology professionals; six others had graduate degrees in fields that included biochemistry, English, communication, and management. I asked them about their initiation into the world of food, motivations for blogging, and the types of cooking they write about. The bloggers seemed ready to share their experiences of blogging and living in the United States and, in one case, in the UK.

The diasporic bloggers are part of a growing social world of women who are situating themselves and their food blogs within the digital space of other Indian food blogs and within the greater world of food blogs at large. I will describe how the bloggers shape the textualization of Indian food by highlighting its diversity and flexibility. The blog posts construct diasporic gendered culinary publics through (1) remembering the culinary textures of localities, (2) promoting the global malleability of Indian cuisine, and (3) navigating the politics and materiality of gendered transnational lives.

## Places lived and remembered

### Homeland

The turn to region and locality is very central to the bloggers in their contextualization of food practices. In the vignettes that emerge about themselves and their blog sites, diasporic bloggers establish their commitment to representing the foods of specific locales associated with their past. Instead of the stereotypical representations of Indian cuisine, the bloggers strive to showcase regional food within its relational and social context. Affective involvement and identification with regions are conflated with Indianness. Consider, for example, the sensory details and relational framing of regional cooking offered here by Sandeepa:

> My blog . . . is a collection of Bengali Recipes representing the Bengali Cuisine as I know it. It also has those recipes that are non-Bengali but which we loved. The measurements are not always exact as I do not treat the kitchen as a lab but as a place where I follow my heart and rely on my senses and instinct.[6]

Sharing culinary knowledge is linked to the desire to recreate the natural foods associated with the uncontaminated simplicity of distant localities.

> I grew up near the beautiful banks of the river Godavari . . . one of the most fertile lands present and is rich in Coconut trees, Mango groves and Paddy fields . . . I have always had a great passion for cooking and enjoying food. I like to experiment and flavorise my dishes with a touch of Indian spices.

> After my marriage I moved to USA and came across lots of new kinds of veggies and fruits that I had never seen before. This gave much thrill and excitement to my cooking as I learnt to Indianise these Western veggies.[7]

Another blogger highlights nature, antiquity, and places in India that have endured.

> Mahanandi is a beautiful temple town close to Nandyala, India and at the foothills of Nallamala forest range. Surrounded by lush forest, fresh water pools and gentle streams, the centuries old temple Mahanandi has a great influence on me. I grew up in Nandyala, and visited Mahanandi many times with my family and have memorable experiences of a life time. The name Mahanandi always evokes calm, content and happy feelings for me. We are made of the places where we lived, the food we ate and the people we interacted with. This website, Mahanandi, is a way for me to show my gratitude to all those what I am made of, the places, the food and the people.[8]

The evocation of rivers and tranquility restores a cultural context to the family meal in a transplanted context. One blogger honors the traditions and hospitality of the Kongu region, where now the waters of the Cauvery river run polluted. In contrast, she celebrates the clean, majestic Potomac and the energy of the new location.

> The Cauvery River and its slow deterioration has shaped my views on the environment. With ancestors who were farmers my mind is never farther from the river. From a vibrant clean river that I was familiar with during my childhood to the dirty polluted river of today, Cauvery is a fine example of environmental degradation. Today, I am fortunate to be living near another majestic river – the Potomac. The Potomac River and the Chesapeake Bay continues to remind me everyday of how clean waterways and healthy fish populations are intertwined with the health and wealth of the people who populate the region.[9]

To the diaspora, India emerges as both pristine and overwhelming.

> Familiar smells ranged from the aromas of different regional cuisines that wafted from open kitchen windows, to the grimy sweat of the relentless crowds, to the lingering metallic odor of trains and buses on my hands and my clothes, to the fishy rotting stench of the bay. I have not missed any of these smells except for the first. I make it a point to have those endearing aromas fill my kitchen on a regular basis.[10]

Delicate aromas and smells of revulsion mingle as regions are recalled through the senses. As Seremetakis (1994: 29) writes, "no smell is encountered alone. There are combinations of smells that make up a unified presence."

## Of places, borders, and segues

Food blogs use the strategy of sharing stories and posting personal preambles to transition into the recipes. Used skillfully by seasoned bloggers, the smooth segue is where questions of difference and identity are introduced and continued in the reader responses. The bridging narratives capture the ways in which diasporic negotiations with food connect regions, memories, and cultural borders.

> Two years back, when I reached Uncle Sam's country, I was really nervous just like anybody who lands in a new place. I knew there won't be many Indians in the place we were going to live. For the same reason, I thought there won't be any Indian groceries either. It was a great relief when I saw spinach on our first trip to the grocery store. Like a flash of lightning this idea struck, "Why not make spinach *thoran* instead of *cheera thoran*."[11]

The subject of parenting in the diasporic context takes center stage as preamble material, eliciting the most responses from readers. The complexity of making the contents of a school lunch box acceptable to "other" children is the subject of much tension in South Asian homes. One blogger launches on the diasporic politics of the school lunch in order to introduce a recipe for a sandwich that can beat the test of ridicule:

> Yeow. That stinks. What's that green stuff? It's disgusting. What's cauliflower? Why is it yellow? That's just gross ... The disgusting green stuff is usually cilantro chutney or baby spinach. The result? She stopped taking chutney-cheese sandwiches – which she simply adores – for lunch.[12]

The blogger Manisha continues that since then the only lunch-worthy Indian foods, to her daughter, are those without any trace of turmeric, ginger, or garlic. A recipe for one such sandwich fluidly follows. A steady stream of responses emerged from women who commiserated, and shared their own parental stories about the crises over Indian lunch, relating it to local parochialism and prejudice.

> Also, the other children's responses are based in their ignorance, due to lack of someone (parents) teaching them that it is not okay to make remarks like that about what someone is eating. I always have to wonder about the parent's attitudes toward people who are different, not like them. Even though you live in a cosmopolitan area, not everyone is cosmopolitan.[13]

The bloggers suggest that due to their global relocations, they have acquired a sense of gastronomic openness, which they equate to a lived cosmopolitanism. Some of the preambles in the diasporic blogs echo the same sense of advocacy that Appadurai (1988) saw in the cookbooks of the 1970s when authors based in India promoted the foods of particular regions. A blogger from Canada uses the common mainstream complaint that Indian food is complicated to make as a segue to a series of recipes and collected tips:

> Now before you roll your eyes at me and say, "Yea sure, easy for you, you're Indian!" just hear me out. True, I was born Indian in an Indian household with a Mom who cooks the most delicious Indian food I know. But truth be told, and as much as I would like to believe, I wasn't born with Indian culinary instincts in me. Yes, like any of you not familiar with the South-Asian cuisine, I too started off without much knowledge . . .Try as I might, somehow, I can't convince people enough on just how simple and quick and not to mention, healthy, Indian food can be. So here is where my mind got to work.[14]

This popular series of highly critical posts, Intro to Indian, has been picked up as a monthly column in a local Canadian newspaper. US-based blogger Manisha, of the very popular and long-standing blog Indian Food Rocks, describes her "pet peeves" about misrepresentations of India and Indian food with alerts such as "*dal* is not a soup" or "people, Indian not east Indians." Asserting that the term "east Indian" is incorrect when describing people from India, Manisha writes: "Accord us the respect we deserve instead of addressing us with qualifiers that reek of colonialism, another form of slavery."[15] There is a strong sense of borders and boundaries that extends into the digital world and sets apart the subculture of the South Asian food blogosphere from the food blogosphere at large.

While the main goal of the bloggers, who mostly write for others in the diaspora, is to reclaim the regional integrity of Indian food, it is clear that many want their blogs to circulate widely. In the next section, I present some bloggers who strive to reach beyond the diaspora. Overall, the recipes and posts about domestic and diasporic themes are gaining visibility in the digital space at large. The social traffic enabled by widgets, blogrolls, memes, and the powerful logic of algorithms accelerates the constitution of this mediated global collectivity.

## Culinary flexibility

The blogs that are read and linked by a broader audience in the greater digital domain are the ones offering recipes attuned to the so-called "modern" palate. I next discuss three blogs whose presentation of the cuisine through the modalities of fusion/adaptability and speed/precision wins the endorsement of wider food circles.

## Fusion and adaptability

Hybrid recreations of Indian food like the tandoori quesadilla or the curry naanwich are the trendy newcomers in global Indian cuisine. To Niv, who specializes in innovations, fusion was a natural extension of the melding of regional cuisines that she had experienced growing up in urban India. The experimentations arose from finding compromises and adaptive shortcuts for Indian food in her American kitchen. For instance, she used a waffle iron to make a south Indian *vadai* and, while the end product might look and feel different, she vouches it is 100 percent authentic. Incorporating filo pastry, wonton wrappers, waffle irons, and ricotta cheese, Niv has added 91 recipes to the popular website Food 52. As she told me, "it's my way of taking Indian food to mainstream America."[16] Her recipe fusing an Indian carrot *halwa*[17] with a blondie bar was accepted by the Cooking Channel and, according to Niv, with the telling comment: "We never expected to pick a dessert in the Indian category."[18] Her fusion recipes, which respond to the stereotypical criticism that Indian desserts are too sweet and lack visual appeal, have drawn varied traffic to her blog, Panfusine.

Framing the image of Indian food in registers of activism, the blog Holy Cow offers Indian vegan food with a global twist and includes

> lots of fat-free, low-fat and gluten-free recipes, and some chatter about the wonderfulness of animals (especially mine :)). Most of my recipes are ideal for those of you who, like me, juggle home and a full-time career but love a delicious and nutritious meal that's also easy to prepare at the end of a long day. But don't just expect a recipe – I like telling you the stories behind the food I serve up.[19]

With the playful title and chatty style, the blog constructs a flexible image of Indian food, one that is cosmopolitan and adaptive to current trends in healthful eating. To blogger Vaishali, vegetarianism is a lifestyle choice and not something prescribed by tradition or religion. There is an easy mingling of regional, vegan Indian fare with other global cuisines. These images of Indian food, as being amenable to innovative transformations, revise its stereotype of being laborious and move it to the threshold of global modernity and a digitally revised diasporic cosmopolitanism.

## Speed and precision

Terminologies that traditional cooks use such as the pinch, a drop, or a handful are now translated into cup measures and forms of precise reproducibility that "other" readers would appreciate. Grandmothers in India are made to sit in front of laptops and video cameras and go through the steps of traditional recipes. Visiting mothers and mothers-in-law are routinely

asked to prepare dishes that are then recast in the language of precise measures and steps – the language of gastro modernity. To UK-based Mallika,
her blog Quick Indian Cooking is a passionate project to set right the
perception of Indian food:

> I started the blog after getting really quite frustrated and annoyed at people's
> perception about Indian food and curry. Culturally it was quite abhorrent to
> me . . . because I'm Indian and have lived in the west for a very long time.
> Unlike a lot of second and third generation Indians, I have grown up in India
> and my connections with India are very strong. It is a misnomer, – there is
> no such thing as Indian food . . . much of what is known as Indian food in
> London is really Pakistani or Bangladeshi.[20]

The blog, written with panache, showcases a global Indian woman who
"you know, can bake the cupcakes over the weekend and is ready to roll
out a presentation for Monday morning."[21] Confessing that she had never
cooked till she came to London to study, she repeats the mantra that you
don't have to slave over a hot stove to cook an Indian meal. In the book *Miss
Masala*, which emerged from the success of the blog, the author describes
herself as "a 30-something girl about town, corporate superbitch and keen
Indian cook" (Basu, 2010: 9). To her large following of young professionals (mainly in the US), she notes that Indian cooking is, in fact, "blindingly
easy and can be a regular part of frantic lives" (Basu, 2010: 15). To this she
adds a few cautions: "I would rather eat my shoe than make a samosa from
scratch. And . . . making round, fluffy *rotis* plays havoc with manicured
fingernails" (Basu, 2010: 8).

*Miss Masala*, hailed by the media in the subcontinent as a sort of Indian
*Bridget Jones's Diary*,[22] offers a discourse about food, consumption, post-
feminism, and diaspora lite. "Daily slaving over a steaming pot simply
wasn't for me. The goddess in me needed shortcuts" (Basu, 2010: 32). Miss
Masala does not identify herself with the curry houses and the insularity
of South Asian immigrants but projects herself as the new global Indian
woman –"a far cry," as she writes, from the "handloom-cotton image I had
of aunties and seasoned cooks back home" (Basu, 2010: 7). Her blog and
now book have a following in India, signaling new connections between the
nation and its non-resident citizen blogger. Using the neoliberal registers of
a trendy cosmopolitanism, she effectively inserts the culture of Indian food
into the demands of a fast-paced global lifestyle with playful tips on how to
"juggle your masalas with your mascaras" (Basu, 2010: cover notes).

## *Gendered politics and mobile texts*

While these diaristic reflections circulate in digital space, they are also tethered to the materiality and gendered politics of transnational diasporic life. Many bloggers mention how friends help with the "tech" stuff and spouses routinely get involved in the photography and tasting. Others talk about their compulsive checking for responses to their posts.

> I check blog comments on my phone when I actually should be finger-painting with the littlest one. Yes, the last one clearly proves I am a blog addict. So to be a better Mother, I need to become calmer – count from 1 to 100 when irritation strikes, fitter – get exercise to build energy and get over my blog addiction – How? Blogging gives me a high like few other thing does and is the only thing I do in my free time (which btw is after 10pm on weekdays and some days at lunch in work). I get immense happiness putting together a post, photo-shopping and writing. I get to be creative by my own rules and often think my life would have a big void if I did not blog. I also love just fleeting from one blog to another and nosing around in total stranger's lives. Sounds like a crack addict? Well almost.[23]

These expressions and interactions in the blogs are shaped by the particularities of the digital space or the socio-technical assemblage from which they arise (see Van Doorn, 2011). The diasporic performances are being constructed within predominantly entrepreneurial enclosures of the blog space where various media forms converge. In my small sample of 13 bloggers, two – Basu (2010) and Datta (2013) – are published authors of successful cookbooks.

During the time I was conducting my interviews, a blogger in India, R, who wrote under the name Miri, died after a long illness. The diasporic culinary blogosphere went into mourning and pledged to cook her recipes in her memory. One of the bloggers actually helped Miri moderate her comments during her illness.

> So I think R actually almost symbolizes a lot of us, where we develop relationships over the Internet and we are not bogged down or held back . . . in R's case the Internet allowed her to be who she was although her body was not letting her. She was in India, this support system is all over the world, we are talking on Facebook, we are sending each other emails, there are some who did not know she was ill . . . One of the reasons we connected was because we grew up in Bombay and loved street food.[24]

The death of R became a focal point, a catalyst for the community to mourn, connect, and renew their commitment to digital activity. While they lamented that they had just learnt that her real name was R, they celebrated the fact that she blogged about recipes from all over the world while still in India. While most of them had never met her in real life, there was a shared understanding that they knew her well through her blog and recipes. Miri's food in turn perpetuates the cultural work of remembrance.

While locations and geographies shape these blogs, so too does the economy. While the bloggers repeatedly note that the blogs are hobbies or activities that they engage in for fun, their closely tracked content produces value for the digital economy (see Terranova, 2000: 35). In addition, the material conditions of their lives are dependent on the demands of economic globalization for the flow of labor from India. As a result of outsourcing, globalization, and the postcolonial emphasis on technical education, Indians account for a very high number of skilled foreign workers in the West. Some bloggers themselves attribute the explosion of food blogs among young women in the United States to a backlash against immigration policies and nested systems of local and global patriarchy. While many of the bloggers self-identify as software or information professionals, the global circuits of information workers are highly gendered. It is mainly men who travel to the United States as skilled economic migrants on H-1B visas, whereas their dependent spouses (on H-4 visas) are not permitted to work, get driver's licenses, or even in some states get a social security number as identification (Uma Devi, 2002).[25] There is much anecdotal conjecture from the media (Challapalli, 2006), from the diasporic community, and from my own respondents that many women who are on an H-4 visa and don't have authorization to work begin to blog. The visa issue is typically not discussed, but here is one exception:

> While there is a strong lobby for illegal immigrants, the general populace is unaware of what an H4 spouse undergoes in terms of isolation from society: can't work, can't drive, is totally dependent. Winter is a daunting prospect when the days are cold and dark. If the Indian food blogs that are emerging are a fallout of this situation, then that is something very positive that is happening. Because even if the women are physically alone at home, they are virtually connected or are connecting with one another through very strong bonding agents, culture and food. That is very comforting.[26]

Predictably, the cuisine has gained more global visibility than many of the women bloggers who move with their families following the pathways of capital. The recipes now travel faster than the people who write them.[27] The blogs, by and large, avoid political discussions and choose instead to remain as stylistic spaces of culinary display and domestic reflections.

# Conclusion

Mobilizing the familiar and banal through the use of image, text, and formats, the food blogs examined here reflect and shape diasporic life and identifications in the global neoliberal context. The digital practices of place-making create diasporic environments that are both "privately public and publicly private" (Papacharissi, 2010: 142). Using interactive modalities and synchronous communication across borders, the blogs fill the spatial gaps and temporal disconnects that have historically clinched the isolation of the diasporic experience. Instead, the bloggers establish a transnational circuit of exchange, a dynamic connection with their country of origin that is no longer a lost homeland, consigned to nostalgia, but represents "a generative living source of knowledge and history" (Kun, 2004: 744).

While media technologies are influential, they work within the parameters of the normative social order. Gender roles and social hierarchies that frame the diasporic locations are reaffirmed, for the most part, with conviviality. The blogs construct webs of affiliation between women but within a tiered system of popularity and visibility. Collectively, the bloggers actively link the cuisine with a diasporic brand of cosmopolitanism and, in the process, recalibrate the regional politics of Indian food for consumption in the global context. This tethering of cuisine to the cultural lives of the diaspora is significant, since typically cultural products from India circulate in the global marketplace delinked from their quotidian cultural contexts.[28]

The food blogs reveal a mediatic shift in the nature of diasporic culture, community, and connectivity. The interesting fact is not that diasporic groups are using new or newer media but rather how the very conditions of connectivity are transforming the meaning of how communities are formed. First of all, the blogs with the affordances of converging media technologies enable a sustained connection with the homeland and the enactment of a flexible mode of cosmopolitan nationalism. Next, this cultural work occurs within an entrepreneurial frame of communicative capitalism (Dean, 2010), where every recipe and post is likely to be counted or rated for its popularity and circulatory muscle. A steady filtering of content and community occurs through both authorial and automated processes. While on the surface, a vibrant, likeminded diasporic community seems to emerge organically, it is to a large extent coaxed into formation (Lampa, 2004) and regulated by algorithms, aggregators, and other technical manipulations. The blogs capture the digital reimagination and production of a strategically distributed version of diasporic publics, embedded within the market logics of a digital economy and a culture of individuation. This merging of a neoliberal ethos and technology shifts the register of discussion about both food and diaspora. While publics, as Warner (2002: 8) argues, exist only by virtue of their imagining, global mobility, media, and market logics set the context for transnational communities to be actualized. In terms of both food practices and community, the blogs represent the active work of consolidation by diasporic bloggers who strategically network and keep track of each other's textual and digital movements.

# 6 Authenticity: Pursuits of Auras

The presence of the original is the prerequisite to the concept of authenticity.
Benjamin, 1968: 220

In the contested cultural spaces of diasporic lives, the notion of authenticity exerts considerable symbolic power. Evocations of the real or the original initiate a series of cultural demands that make and unmake ethnic identities. Upheld as a normative model, the authentic not only scripts expectations, but also reins in what is considered inauthentic. The tension between the copy and the original sustains the idea of the authentic, as theorized by Benjamin (1968). This tension gains material significance in the context of diasporic cultures where identities are subject to intense scrutiny and protocols of authentication. In immigrant neighborhoods situated in global cities, such as Astoria, Kreuzberg, or Southall,[1] there are frequent references to the notion of authenticity. For example, it is common to see street signage urging one to savor experiences like "the real tastes of Lebanon," "the true sounds of Brazil," "true Turkish hospitality," or even "authentic Indian bliss." In Lakhous' (2006) novel about immigrants in Rome, *Clash of Civilizations Over an Elevator in Piazza Vittorio*, the Iranian refugee Parviz cooks the delicacies of his homeland in order to connect with his past. As the various aromas of spices waft around, Parviz says, "the odors that fill the kitchen make me forget reality and I imagine that I've returned to my kitchen in Shiraz" (Lakhous, 2006: 19). Cooking connects Parviz on many different levels to the real Shiraz in Iran, which, as Lakhous notes with great insight, Parviz has never left. Mediating the connections between cultural practices, everyday life, discourses, and ideologies, a vision of the authentic mandates forms of conformity or spurs inventive ways of reworking tradition. An imagined certainty about the original and a stable image of an ideal form are intrinsic to the concept of authenticity (Lowney, 2009).

As I wrote this chapter, global audiences were focused on the 2014 World Cup and soccer mania was in the air. The intensity of the fans and conspicuous displays of patriotism around the games were reminders of the close links that have historically existed between sports, nationalism, and the showing of a "true" brand of patriotism. When Algeria qualified for the knockout stages of the World Cup for the first time, Algerian immigrants took to the streets in France to cheer this landmark event. The celebration in June 2014 was met swiftly with a stern response and disciplinary action from local authorities. The mayor of the French city of Nice banned what he considered ostentatious waving of foreign flags, stating that the city could not accept these excesses of behavior.[2] To Marine Le Pen, the leader of the far-right National Front party in France, the soccer affiliations of the Algerian immigrants were a clear indication of the failure of the French immigration system and the refusal of binationals to assimilate. She stated emphatically in an interview: "They must choose: they are Algerian or French, Moroccan or French, they can't be both."[3] Clearly this is not such a simple decision as it is made out to be. The binational affiliations of immigrants cannot be dismissed so easily, and especially in this case, they are related to the complex histories and geographies of colonial entanglements that continue to connect Algeria and France. Even such innocuous expressions by immigrants gain political valence, and are measured by normative standards of what are considered authentic expressions of citizenship. The authentic here assumes an exclusionary logic used to identify and filter out inauthentic citizens who cannot express the right kind of nationalism. The earlier chapter on veiling referred to similar expectations of authentic performances of national belonging.

Comments on public excitement about soccer and citizenship were predictably made in the United States as well. Ann Coulter, a conservative political commentator, characterized the new interest in soccer as being foreign and un-American. In her column, Coulter attributed the new American interest in soccer to demographic shifts caused by immigration: "I promise you: No American whose great-grandfather was born here is watching soccer. One can only hope that, in addition to learning English, these new Americans will drop their soccer fetish with time."[4] These are but recent iterations of old scripts and outbursts against immigration and about the appropriate and authentic displays of citizenship in the arena of sports. In 1990, Norman Tebbit, a Conservative member of Parliament in the UK, questioned the patriotism of South Asian immigrants who did not cheer for the British cricket team, but supported India or Pakistan instead. In an interview with the *Los Angeles Times*, Tebbit proposed a cricket test for immigrants: "Which side do they cheer for? It is an interesting test. Are you still harking back to where you came from or where you are? I think we have got real problems in that regard."[5]

These various examples demonstrate that even the most banal of everyday practices of immigrants have historically been scrutinized, and continue to be judged according to what are considered authentic standards of performing citizenship. While nebulous and slippery, authenticity is still routinely claimed as a fixed concept and in turn attached to strict definitions of cultural forms, valorizing, as Weiss (2011) writes, origins, hierarchies, and certitudes. The boundaries between the true citizen and the Other are erected along very rigid forms of culture and cultural affiliations that are at odds with the mobile ways in which people live and identify in the liquid context of globalization (Bauman, 2006). This recurring tension has been a focal point in the various sites explored in this book. Given that the culture of diasporic communities is in continual flux, notions of authenticity, being discursively constructed, are also both contingent and contested. Debates about authenticity flow swiftly from the sensory, aesthetic, and affective realm into the economic and political. For example, a sensational conspiracy that took place in the New York art scene captures how the world of capital shapes both diasporic life and the category of the authentic.

In August 2013, Pei-Shen Qian, an immigrant from China, made headlines in the media as the artist behind a multimillion-dollar forgery scam that shook the international art scene. According to media reports, Qian, working from his garage in Queens, New York, had produced at least 63 drawings and paintings that carried the signatures of great painters, including Jackson Pollock, Mark Rothko, and Robert Motherwell. The art dealers who had discovered Qian sold the paintings as newly found work of these famous artists to galleries in New York City.[6] Experts have been both perplexed and amazed by the skill and talent of a painter who could produce copies that were indistinguishable from the originals, even to trained eyes. Qian, who has been named "the Times Square faker" by the media, made a few thousand dollars on each of his fakes, which raked in millions of dollars for the conspiring dealers.[7] He is reported to have stumbled on his own reproduction in an art show, when he realized how little he was making on the forgery. The scheme was discovered when an art collector tried to have one of the so-called Pollock paintings authenticated and found that it was a fake. Indicted for fraud, Qian has since fled to Shanghai where he now lives and paints. He claims that he always believed that his fakes were sold as copies and did not know that they were being passed off as the real thing.

Qian's own life was a tough pursuit of the elusive ideal of the immigrant dream, the dream so singularly captured in the United States as an individual tale of hard work and the ascent to success. Before coming to the United States, he is said to have been part of a small group of artists in China who, by some accounts, rekindled the Shanghai art scene.[8] Once in New York, he experienced a loss in status (as many immigrants do) and worked as a janitor, a construction worker, and a painter to survive in the global city. His talent was noticed while he was hustling tourists to get their portraits painted in New York City's Times Square. In an interview with the *New*

*York Times,* another Chinese painter in New York mentioned that Qian was frustrated and isolated to a large extent because of the language barrier. Media reports indicate that Qian was deeply disheartened that he had not found his niche in New York's art scene.[9] While no doubt he is implicated in the conspiracy, the case highlights the locational politics of immigrant life and labor. It is ironic that Qian's artistic talent and his worth as an artist are tied to the continued invisibility of his immigrant labor as a painter of fakes.

The story raises a number of questions about the perception of authenticity and assumptions about how it is to be defined, evaluated, and even performed. The sensational story frames the centrality of authenticity in the aesthetic domain and the unquestionable aura of the original. At the same time, it also raises another set of questions about the politics of value, the cultural capital of immigrants, the conditions of their visibility, and the continuing nature of transnational ties. The painter Qian's actions have also to be mapped against his survival story as an immigrant and what Spivak (1999: 360) calls "the cultural vicissitudes of migrancy." As a painter and an immigrant, Qian was implicated on many levels in the intertwined calculus of the original and the copy. Woven with multiple plot lines, the narrative launches a discussion about the larger issues concerning the circulation of people and commodities, the production and manipulation of value, and above all, the cultural power of authenticity and its multiple mobilizations.

The tension around authenticity serves as a vantage point from where to think about how the circulatory paths of migrants, cultural forms, and commodity flows merge and gain meaning in the context of the global economy. Conceptualizations of the authentic also fortify boundaries and the distinctions between the margins and centers (Ramos-Zayas, 2003). Authenticity operates as a powerful force that drives the cultural life of immigrants through implicit consensus about not only what constitutes true citizenship, but also identities and performances that contaminate the definition. Working at the level of individual and collective identity, authenticity, according to Lindholm (2007), has two overlapping forms: genealogical or historical (origin) and identity or correspondence (content). He argues that these two modes are not always compatible or invoked equally in every context; however, both stand in contrast to whatever is fake, unreal, or false. It is the imagination of an ideal cultural form or practice that plays a constitutive role in the material shaping of diasporic experiences.[10] Surfacing in assimilative modes to discipline immigrants, the evocation of authenticity often simplifies and naturalizes social, cultural, and even historical phenomena (Mayer, 2012). At other times, authenticity appears in a civilizational register where old traditions, defined in essentialist terms, are revived (and

89

prescribed) in the nostalgic spirit of preserving culture. Finally, there is the more inventive mode where the idea of the authentic drives innovative ways of navigating and producing cultural connections between home, nation, and tradition. The notion of authenticity is intricately connected to new media technologies, commodities, and the world of the market – a conjuncture that has gained both value and visibility in the context of neoliberal globalization. Not only do digital technologies reproduce the original with high standards of fidelity, they also paradoxically claim that the reproduction is more real than the original. The claim resonates with the diaspora who, in the process of re-territorializing and recreating traditions, also try to outdo the original.

This chapter will discuss how an assemblage of interconnected transnational factors shape the ways in which cultural reproduction takes place in the lives of diasporic communities. I unravel the term "authenticity" and contestations over the real from a number of differing angles in order to demonstrate how the diaspora, defined by a web of social relations, negotiate their performative worlds. Diasporic life today is shaped between and across borders by a series of political, economic, and technological transformations. As Purkayastha (2009: 87) notes, these transnational experiences are not entirely separable from nation-based experience; rather, these "encounters *interact and intersect* with experiences within countries of residence to deepen, dilute, and/or change the experiences of diasporic groups." These global connections are accelerated by the neoliberal digital economy, ever alert to remaking diasporic longings into market opportunities, leveraging, of course, the appeal of the authentic. The social worlds of a specific subset of South Asian immigrants, and their transnational involvement in the traditional performing arts of India, serve as a case study from which to discuss how the cultural economy of authenticity is driving a networked diasporic experience. Weiss (2011: 77) argues that the proper question to ask is not, "Is it authentic?" but rather, "How is it authentic?" The coming together of the digital and diasporic pushes this question and the politics of authenticity further.

## Negotiating Auras

There is a great deal of investment from various quarters in keeping the allure of the authentic alive. When it comes to nationalism, as seen in the sports example, authenticity is deployed in order to raise ideological boundaries and demarcate those who rightfully belong as a citizen. In the domain of the aesthetic, authenticity rests on the materiality of the original, its timeless appeal, and the circumstances of its creation. In the realm of consumerism, the worth or sign value of the commodity or object is tied firmly to its authenticity (Baudrillard, 1998) and processes of authentication by experts. Clearly the power of the authentic plays a transformative role across social and cultural contexts by certifying provenance and evoking appropriate affect (Lindholm, 2007).[11] There continues to be an increasing focus on authenticity in the context of the digital media, whose signature processes are reproduction, replication, and reiteration. The fixed and territorially rooted notion of authenticity is flexed and tested by the global mobility of commodities and people. Reworking the authentic is part of the emergence of different types of cultural forms. For example, writing about popular culture and its relationship to the ideology of authenticity, Grossberg (1992: 208) argues that for a cultural form like rock and roll to survive, "it must seek to reproduce its authenticity in new forms, in new places and in new alliances."

The quest for authenticity ultimately rests on the perception of the singular and ineffable aura of the original, which Walter Benjamin (1968) has famously argued is itself in decline due to the proliferation of reproductive technologies. The pursuit of the authentic and the emergence of an industry around its preservation are driven by the impending fact of the disintegration of the aura. Aura, according to Benjamin's (1968: 222) definition, is "the unique phenomenon of distance, however close it may be." However, while the notion of aura is most commonly associated with the aesthetic, Benjamin implies that genuine aura appears in all things. Arguing that Benjamin's deployment of aura and its historical shifts are part of his effort to reconceptualize experience under technologically mediated conditions, Hansen (2008: 342) notes that aura is not an inherent property of persons or objects, but rather an in-between substance that mediates and constitutes meaning.

Benjamin (1968) makes the point that any analysis of art in the age of mechanical reproduction must take into consideration that the work of art reproduced becomes the work of art designed for reproducibility. Since reproduction, according to Benjamin, emancipates art from ritual, art itself changes in order to be reproduced. In a similar way, one could argue that cultural traditions are now being reworked transnationally with reproducibility in mind, as these older cultural forms are commodified for global consumption and circulated as digital avatars. These reformulated traditions are designed with a view to having portable auras, which not only survive the multiplicity of copies, but also are made for it. What emerge, then, are inventive, sometimes resistant ways of defining culture and the terms of its portability. In the diaspora, digitally enabled recreations of old traditions both complicate and manipulate the meaning of the real and authentic.

Being mobile, fluid, and globally connected, diasporic cultures cannot be treated as self-contained. Cultural borders between communities have always been porous and are even more so today, thereby transnationalizing the horizon of everyday life. While diasporic communities reproduce familiar practices, they also establish distinct performative modes of their own which are neither wholly mimetic, nor simple additive versions of other cultural forms. Instead, as Kun (2004) points out in his rich study of the urban musical culture of Mexican Los Angeles, music born of migration and globalization responds to circuits of cultural flow and at the same time also shapes what global culture looks and sounds like. Yet these mobile processes are often described in essentialized terms, as though static, pure, and fixed to specific places. When it comes to talking about ethnic minorities, according to Raj (2003), there is a tendency to be caught in a conceptual straitjacket formed by assumptions that migrants bring *a* culture from the homeland, that ethnic culture is a transitory phenomenon, and finally that ethnic minorities will assimilate. In contrast, these cultures are dynamic forms articulated and performed at the nexus of technological change, global economic flows, and desire. Appadurai (1996: 13) writes that culture is not usefully regarded as a substance, but should rather be regarded as a situated and embodied dimension of phenomena: "Stressing the dimensionality of culture rather than its substantiality permits our thinking of culture less as a property of individuals and groups and more as a heuristic device that we can use to talk about difference." I use this suggestion to frame the diaspora's fluid reproduction of the nation, its auras and perceived authenticities, with the help of communication and digital technologies.

While the notion of authenticity is related to value and the commodity form, it is also registered in the realm of the senses. When the diaspora and the nation connect, cultural reproduction is mediated through the sensorium. Digital forms of cultural reproduction in the diaspora are leading to new forms of organizing sensory perception. In the next section I discuss how the diaspora reclaims the homeland through the reproduction of its soundscapes. Diasporic communities resort to the power of technology to enable the production, transmission, and performance of authentically traditional sounds. At the same time, the possibility of forging new authenticities with the use of newly available digital interfaces presents the diaspora as a social and economic opportunity for the nation. With diasporic communities being perceived as an important consumer group, selling traditions to them has become a profitable global enterprise. This is not the diaspora severed from the homeland, but one that is connected to and at the center of a transnational circuit of aesthetic exchange and commodity flows.

## Re-Sounding Authenticity

Once a month on a Sunday, a small crowd gathers outside the Cornelia Street Café, a noted jazz venue located on a side street just off bustling Sixth Avenue in New York City. They are waiting to experience an evening of traditional classical music from southern India, Carnatic music, in a narrow and intimate space. They mostly represent a diverse, urban audience to whom this music and its sounds are a completely new experience. As the evening progresses, this very diverse group is clearly riveted by the music – some swaying in their seats, others moving their bodies to the rhythm. Arun Ramamurthy, a second-generation South Asian American violinist from Brooklyn, New York, is determined to bring these classical Indian sounds to New York City audiences. When I interviewed him about his artistic work in the area of Carnatic music, Arun said enthusiastically: "It's improvisational, complicated, and challenging." He was convinced that jazz audiences in New York City would take to this form of Indian classical music, packaged the right way. Arun curates an ongoing concert series of Indian classical music in this iconic New York City jazz haunt – Carnatic Sundays – which is gaining popularity not only with the diaspora but also with a wider audience across the board. Arun's curatorial coup has added a new authenticity to the urban soundscape of the global city.

What happens when a traditional aesthetic form with its particular

Getting ready for Carnatic Sunday at the Cornelia Street Café in New York City
Image: Trina Basu

93

performative modalities moves to a new locale? When cultural practices are delinked from specific geographies, historical connections between place and culture are interrupted, and the process of re-telling or re-sounding authenticity is orchestrated by the intersection of social and economic factors. Carnatic music, a musical tradition originating in south India, is typically performed observing strict traditional codes that match the spirituality that suffuses this particular musical form. Performing Carnatic music in a New York City jazz venue alters the performative dynamics and interactive energy exchanged with the audience. Talking about the Cornelia Street Café performances, Akshay Ananthapadmanabhan, a percussionist and a regular performer in the series, explained to me, "we want to bring a footprint of Carnatic music into the New York City music scene. The series is attracting a different crowd from places outside the Carnatic purview." The musicians, however, were insistent that this did not compromise the authenticity and traditional rigor of their art. Another musician from New York City, vocalist Roopa Mahadevan, for instance, mentioned that preserving the classical spirit of Carnatic music and making it available to a new audience take considerable work. It required strategic planning about the presentation and firm decisions regarding aesthetic choices concerning the songs and melodies performed. The pieces they would select for a New York City audience, largely unexposed to Indian classical music, would be very different from ones they would select for a South Asian diasporic audience, or for an audience in India. As the singer Roopa told me, reworking a traditional art form for a new audience definitely required "a certain amount of tweaking" of the various elements. Interestingly, she also added, "you have to reconsider some of the elements without compromising the authenticity of the framework." The attention to authenticity is ever present, although its meaning remains fluid and negotiable.

The global circulation of Indian classical music has been dramatically reorganized by the increasing visibility of the Indian diaspora in the West, its desire to be connected aurally to the nation, and the presence of converging media technologies. Indian classical music, especially the Carnatic style of southern India, is currently being actively reinvented for the global stage by dispersed transnational networks of actors and institutions. A style that so far has had an audience base mainly from the four southern states of India is now fashioning itself as a global cultural product by leveraging tradition to stake its claim on a global future. The diaspora, with its longing to retain the cultural gloss of high culture from the homeland, serves as the perfect context for the global emplacement of Carnatic music. The cultural capital of Carnatic music and its relationship to a historical sense of identity are actively recreated in North America with a special emphasis on maintaining cultural and aesthetic fidelity. The sonic landscape of migrant long-ings provides an opening for new technological opportunities to bridge the nation and its diaspora through the audible entanglement (Guilbaut, 2005) of performance, transmission, audiences, and social relations.

As mentioned earlier, new forms of technological connectivity have rede-fined the experience of migration by offering, as Appadurai (1996) notes, new resources for self-making and self-imagining. For the South Asian dias-pora, digital technology, especially communication platforms and forms of social media, have opened up possibilities of immersion in the aesthetics of Indian classical music. The Internet and communication platforms like Skype offer digital spaces where the diasporic communities from southern India are connecting performatively with classical forms of expressive cul-ture. Instructors of classical music in India are reaching diasporic students through pedagogical styles that rest on the potential of communication technology to combine formats and to transcend time zones and spatial boundaries. The technology-enabled pedagogy and its various digital acces-sories respond in novel ways by yoking diasporic desires to preserve tradi-tion and the global identity of the music itself. What used to be primarily a local, oral, and face-to-face tradition in India is now being redesigned by and for the diaspora to incorporate new forms of mediation, transnational participation, and digital coordination.

This digital energy in the area of music is synchronous with India riding the wave of global technological visibility and the growing presence of Indian immigrants in the professional high-tech sectors in the West. Examining the musical ambitions of this community reveals the mediated shifts that are taking place in the cultural connections between the diaspora and the nation.[12] These digitally enabled diasporic leanings toward authen-tic versions of classicism have set in motion some interesting trends – global technologization of the Carnatic (south Indian) style of classical music, the creation of new audiences, and the refashioning of aural traditions. The diaspora and the nation both participate from very distinct positions in shaping the portability of traditions and chalking out a global itinerary for the travel of authentic classical music.

## Identity as Cultural Literacy

The South Asian diaspora, as van der Veer (1995) notes, is far from a trans-parent category, as it encapsulates varied global histories and trajectories.[13] In the wake of global trends in the information technology industry and the participation of India in the knowledge industry, there has been a sharp increase in the circulation of skilled migrants. With the demand for Indian software programmers in Europe, Australia, and the US during the dot.com boom, the South Asian diaspora has gained a prominent digital presence (Gajjala, 2010). This narrative of diaspora is being shaped by the intersecting energies of this skilled migrant community, capital, technology, and a dominant belief in cultural literacy as a prerequisite to the performance of true Indianness.

Music and dance of both classical and popular traditions are central to the cultural life and mediascape of Indian immigrants, and the reproduction of these bodies of knowledge is linked to the enactments of Indianness. As Shukla (2003: 216) writes, "a very old question, of what is Indian, less Indian, more Indian, and still Indian appears as the quality of Indianness becomes unmoored from nation, state, or any other mechanism of surveillance."[14] The identity calculation of what constitutes the right amount and texture of Indianness is often established in terms of the performing arts and cultural literacy. While there is a strong move among South Asian or *desi* youth to articulate racial identity through alternative forms of artistic expression like rap and hip-hop,[15] there is a simultaneous push and pressure from parents to connect to the musical traditions and heritage of India. Prashad (2000: 115) argues that ethnic events encourage a kind of cultural literacy where "culture operates less in the anthropological sense, as 'what we do,' and more in the normative sense, as 'what every person should know'." Civilizational goals drive social events and pedagogical practices that crowd the lives of the South Asian diaspora, as they construct what Rajagopal (2001: 239) calls "an expatriate nationalism."[16]

This link to music is particularly strong with the immigrants from the southern Indian states of Tamil Nadu, Karnataka, Andhra Pradesh, Telangana, and Kerala, who forge conscious connections to the classical forms and spiritual connotations of Carnatic music. Instruction in the performing arts is equated to providing a dose of Indianness to children raised in the West, and is regarded as a form of cultural fortification and investment in forms of Indian high culture. Much of this socialization is also modeled on the style of early training in music and dance that children in middle-class homes in parts of south India are exposed to. Mirroring that activity, there are a number of teachers in the diasporic community offering Carnatic music instruction in the United States for children and adults alike. To preserve religiosity and adherence to traditions, South Asian parents in the diaspora send their children to religious classes, language instruction, music, and/ or dance to build their cultural capital. Many South Asian music students often go to India over the summer months to train and finesse their music skills with a well-reputed teacher or performer. These immigrants are mostly affluent professionals who are networked into the music circles both in the diasporic scene and in India. Over the years, a variety of media forms including audiocassettes, CDs, music videos, and now more interactive forms of media technology have enabled the creation of soundscapes that keep the diaspora aurally connected and transnationally networked.

Each year in spring, over 10,000 South Asians hailing mainly from the southern states of India convene in Cleveland, Ohio to attend a ten-day music festival. The Cleveland Thyagaraja Festival is now considered the largest gathering of Carnatic music listeners outside of India. In response to an Indian journalist's query about the motivation behind this festival, one of the founders of the Cleveland festival, V. V. Sundaram, made an illustrative comment: "'the manner in which U.S.-born Indian children have taken to this movement, their zeal and enthusiasm to keep the Indian arts alive are reasons enough. They are completely charged-up when they meet artistes they only hear about. This festival is for them!' exclaims Sundaram emphatically."[17] As Hansen (1996: 156) notes, this festival is "an example of how cultural performances that are highly specific, and even parochial in their origins can acquire extended layers of meaning as they move into transnational territory." The diaspora labor to recreate the authentic experience of traditional music in their new surroundings, not only in the name of preserving heritage but also to establish themselves in the eyes of the homeland as exemplary cultural citizens who, although living outside of India, have outdone themselves in upholding the authenticity of artistic performance and high culture.

## Digital Classicism

This transnational diasporic interest in the study and preservation of Indian classical music has resulted in strengthening connections between musicians in India and the diaspora. Technology now serves as the conduit that enables this transnational interaction and renews the life and circulation of new soundscapes. While this is nothing novel, the developments are significant when one takes into consideration the shifting contexts of circulation. Spirituality and principles of simple living have been historically regarded as a prerequisite for a true and authentic Carnatic musician. This ethos was reflected in the traditional pedagogical principles of Carnatic music, which existed well into the 1960s in India, where a student served as apprentice to a teacher or guru without monetary considerations. This was considered the authentic Indian mode of teaching. To the aspiring musician, the learning method was to shadow the guru and emulate his style. An art form largely based on improvisation, Carnatic music has survived with minimal written notation and was passed on through oral traditions and forms of transmission. The invocation of tradition and preservation of authenticity have been pivotal to the project of creating an informed public culture around this music (see Subramanian, L., 2008). In this new global phase of the music's development enabled by the diaspora, technology has been completely absorbed into the circulation and pedagogy of the music. The civilizational rationale of protecting tradition is the undisputed motivation for the presence of Carnatic music in the diaspora. New gurus or teachers of music, both within the diaspora and at home base, are now customizing the old teaching methods in digital formats, claiming to capture the aura at its purest.

With this impetus from the diaspora, the austere musical form has now undergone both a media explosion and a market makeover. The global mobility of professional Indian immigrants has accelerated the technological transformation of the music. The world of Carnatic music is now firmly established in digital space and delivers a knowledge base through the convergence of diverse digital technologies. These pioneering innovations in the traditional world of Indian classical music include podcasts, downloads, blogs, audio databases, software to transliterate lyrics from Indian languages, Wiki sites, Twitter feeds, Google groups, and the like. For example, a well-reputed Carnatic vocalist, Sanjay Subrahmanyan, produces a regular podcast and maintains an active blog site. Every episode of his podcast is downloaded at least 1,000 times on an average and a very large number of these are by Indians of the diaspora, mainly in the United States.[18]

A new community of tech-savvy teachers is fast emerging both in the diasporic community and in India to meet the needs of the diaspora. Vidya Subramanian presents an interesting profile of the new musician – an MBA from Boston College, a performing musician, podcaster, and popular online instructor who maintains a website and a presence on Facebook, and attracts a large number of fans from around the world for her podcasts. Through her web presence, Vidya notes that she has heard from new listeners from Thailand, Estonia, and all over the United States. Her mission, she states, is to popularize Carnatic music, globalize its audience base, and develop a repository of podcasts. The ultimate future of her portal depends on her listeners: "We will take it where our listeners want it to go. We really want to create an exciting and non-intimidating experience but don't want to alter anything as far as the traditional boundaries of the music go, but we do want to bring in new listeners."[19] Embedded in this discourse is the certainty of the belief that technology will lift the music enjoyed up to now mainly by audiences from the southern states of India to a global threshold.

The musicians claim that due to the reach of technology, they have succeeded in moving the music, its authenticity intact, to a new cosmopolitan space where they can reach new audiences. A Carnatic musician in Washington DC says: "For the old masters who taught me in the 70s, recording was taboo, they saw it as the looting of their treasures. But for me, the Internet is a billboard, a way to reach a worldwide audience."[20] Others like K. N. Shashikiran have futuristic dreams of creating cultural tech-parks where students can surf around for premium versus regular gurus and the teaching will be conducted on the model of a 24-hour call center.[21] In his blog, Shashikiran states that the days of the old-school music teacher in India, who stereotypically carried an unpretentious bag on his shoulder and gave music lessons to students in their homes, has come to an end. Today the music teachers are "tech-savvy musicians who teach *shisyas* (students) from all over the world, over the Internet! And they don't house-hop anymore, they cyber-trot. From the concept of the *gurukul*,[22] we have progressed to 'guru-cool'."[23]

The Internet is celebrated as offering an instantaneous intervention to open up the exclusive preserves of musical knowledge. In this narrative, there is also a collapsing of other media histories and the slow evolution of musical pedagogy that has progressed through earlier mediated iterations such as instruction using cassette tapes, through radio and television, and even via long-distance telephone calls. Those earlier media forms have in fact cleared the space and created the conditions for this latest remediation. Instead musicians and journalists alike identify the advent of these latest forms of communication technology as signaling a radical paradigm shift in the identity of the music and the musician. In an earlier moment in the postcolonial history of Carnatic music, there was considerable debate about the use of technology, and resistance in particular to the introduction of sound amplifying and recording technologies, including the microphone, gramophone, and radio.[24] Today, due to the driving interest of the diaspora, the musician and the music are now both defined and held together via networked technology. Older forms of music instruction are now deemed provincial and premodern in contrast to the techno frontiers of the customizable, more globally attuned digital pedagogies of the neo-Carnatic scene. Mazzarella (2004: 357) makes a pertinent argument: "as Derrida and other scholars suggest, this constitutive mediation also always produces a fiction of premediated existence."

## Educating the Diaspora

The presence of the diaspora has been the impetus for musicians and music educators in India to revise forms of the traditional pedagogy of Indian classical music. Using technology, instruction is being redesigned to meet the particular demands and tastes of transnational students. These exchanges enable these new forms of mediated instruction and facilitate modes of exchange between the nation and its diaspora (Sugarman, 2004). These digital initiatives undertaken by musicians in India are driven by the desire to recruit diasporic students with their privileged access to global capital and the West. In fact, popular reports allege that the presence of the diaspora is contributing to the global patronage and revival of Carnatic music, which was losing its younger audience base in India to the immense popularity of Bollywood music. As a columnist for an online Indian magazine notes, the obituary of Carnatic music might have to be retracted due to the support from the diaspora, and the epicenters of this classical form might be shifting to New York, Boston, Atlanta, San Francisco, and Toronto.[25]

The conjuncture of diaspora and global technology has enabled particular articulations of musical knowledge that claim immediacy, intimacy, completeness, and authenticity. These claims touch the right note to further diasporic interests to connect with teachers in India through digital means. The diasporic student is seeking authenticity in terms of the music, the pedagogy, and also the expertise of the teacher. The teacher in India, perceived as closer to the tradition, is preferred to the growing but limited choice of teachers available in the West. In addition, to the diasporic parents, online classes simplify the demands of suburban life in the US and offer a convenient alternative to driving children to various extra-curricular classes. To older students, this is the perfect timesaving way to take customized special music lessons while balancing other professional demands on their time. Parents are very proud of being able to arrange for lessons from a "real" *guru* from "back home."

The teachers, in turn, are rescripting their teaching styles to be more in tune with their non-resident students and their mediated environments. Most of the teachers who conduct classes online essentially cater to the diasporic student and run their classes across international time zones like a call center. The presence of an affluent diasporic audience and the potentialities of technology generate labor opportunities. Increasingly, women who are musically inclined and are unable to work outside the home due to the responsibilities of children and family are turning to this form of online teaching. Jayshri Prakash, a musician in Bangalore, told me during an interview conducted via Skype about her home office that she has set up and organized with a computer, headphones, broadband wireless, and a good office chair. No longer does she settle down to teach by sitting on the floor cross-legged, in the traditionally required yogic style. Rather, she is in her ergonomic chair tilted at the right angle for the webcam. "I started off with four students; now I have about 25 students in the US, eight or ten in the UK, four in Australia and two in Singapore." Her day begins very early in the morning so she can teach the students in the eastern United States during their evening hours. Moving longitudinally with the time zones, Jayshri returns after her lunch break to teach her diasporic students mainly on the east coast of the United States, in the New York and New Jersey area. Vidya, the other teacher quoted earlier, noted a similar pattern but also included Thailand, Botswana, and Slovenia in her pedagogical itinerary.

There is overall a high level of enthusiasm among most musicians about the new models of teaching, but always with the required nod to tradition, and the acknowledgment that technology cannot replace the grandeur of our *gurukula* system. Yet there is also the argument that the music has to adapt to the needs of new types of students. Technological glitches, such as a lag or video quality, seem to be the only negatives that are mentioned. Solutions to most problems always involve more gadgetry or new software, both of which are being developed in Bangalore at a brisk pace.[26] The language of the neoliberal economy and marketing finds its way into the discourse and style of these new teachers. Vidya says she has to keep the pedagogy exciting and move away from the beaten path in order to carve out a niche in what is becoming a highly competitive market of online music education. She took a cue from her own exposure to management education and told me during the interview: "If you take a course in the business school, there is a knowledge component and an applied component. You can't focus on derivatives in the first seminar . . . that would be disastrous."

South Asian immigrants, either as students of music themselves or as highly involved parents of students, are perceived by music teachers in India as being very discerning due to their professional and educational background. In addition, the teachers argue that they have to develop new methods that will appeal to the second generation – the children who are often unfamiliar with the language and Indian cultural traditions in which this music is entrenched. Teachers like Vidya Subramanian argue that this new, fast-paced, and innovative approach to Carnatic music is a necessary pedagogical intervention in order to reach this cosmopolitan group.

The fears and desires of the diaspora have traditionally been inscribed on the second generation, and it is obvious in this case as well. In their enthusiasm to instill Indian values directly from the source in India, the parents I talked to in New Jersey mentioned that they make their children sit down in front of the computer for their music lessons via Skype, which happen either early in the morning before school or after eight at night. Parents stress that this is a way to introduce youngsters to the discipline of classical music and that a regular and structured exposure to tradition will ensure its preservation in the diasporic context. The children, who are not always fluent in Indian languages, typically don't understand the lyrics in the music, which are often based on stories from classical Indian mythology. As Jayshri, the teacher in Bangalore mentioned to me during the interview I conducted, said: "I have to teach the American-born children about Indian mythology, so I have to point them to children's books because the stories and the language are so alien to them." The teachers are expected to deliver more than music education and serve as civilizational brokers to the second-generation diasporic students. Overall in India, teaching the diaspora adds a certain global luster to the teacher's résumé.

The language of the marketplace and of self-help has also been added to this pedagogical practice, securing a type of branding trajectory in global economic pathways. To many teachers of music who also maintain an active performance schedule, teaching online is the only option to fit their schedule. In an article in the *Hindu*, a national English-language daily newspaper in India, a very noted and popular performer/teacher, Neyveli Santhanagopalan, writes that the e-guru is there not to eliminate the role of the guru, but to encourage the cultivation of the guru within you – the You-guru.

> Many social, technological and economic developments in today's world are here to stay – it is up to us to channel these changes towards a better future while preserving the rich heritage of the past. The success of an art-form, culture or tradition lies in its ability to integrate with changing times. I see the e-Guru to Guru to You-Guru transitions as a means to integrate our music with today's world.[27]

## Presentations of the Authentic

As the diaspora engages with this new form of Carnatic music education, the discourse of authenticity frequently surfaces as the defining criterion of evaluation. The music, the teachers, and the experience are all judged on the basis of authenticity, which, in turn, was defined by many I spoke to as "something you feel then you know." Authenticity distinguishes the music that is perceived as pure, uncontaminated, and adhering to an unbroken chain of traditional musical renditions. The teachers evoke authenticity to capture the truthful adherence to tradition that they maintain either due to or in spite of the technology. While clearly authenticity is an idiosyncratic yardstick, it still works to loosely identify the value of the teacher and the lesson. For the diaspora, authenticity is the quality that makes the aesthetics and cultural appeal of Indianness both visible and audible. However, the ultimate validation of authenticity for the diasporic musician comes from gaining recognition from the home country. The students who are serious about the music and aspire to being performing artists themselves remain connected with senior musicians in India through technology-enabled lessons. Yet the nation is not so ready or welcoming to its diasporic artists, who have to jump through many hoops to gain recognition as artists in India. The reason hinges precisely on the question of authenticity. There is either a critique on the home front that the bar has been lowered for the diasporic performer, or there is a touch of unrealistic wonder about their accomplishment and its authenticity. After a performance in Chennai, India, by Roopa Mahadevan from New York, a review of the recital in the local newspaper stated: "Considering that she's actually a Stanford University post-graduate in 'cognitive neuroscience,' the absolutely authentic quality of her Carnatic music is truly astonishing!"[28] Ultimately, the validation of the diasporic musician and the adjudication regarding the authenticity of their performance have to come from a teacher, critic, and audiences located in India.

To Sundaram, of the Cleveland Festival of music, the most important goal of the annual Festival is to prepare young diasporic performers in Carnatic classical music. The Cleveland Festival runs a very popular national competition in Carnatic music where many diasporic young performers compete. Sundaram states they will take the winner to India and showcase her talent by saying: "Look at this kid, born and brought up in USA, and is as good as anyone learning traditionally in India."[29] The diasporic location of liminality and the ability to maintain what is perceived as a fine balance of the modern and the traditional is precisely what draws both wonder and resentment from the nation. The balancing act required to hold on to Indianness in new geographies is seen as a demonstration of diasporic tenacity and resilience. One teacher in India even mentioned to me that some of her diasporic students are "more Indian than her Indian students." This notion of non-resident Indian students being more Indian than Indians is quite commonly circulated in India.[30]

The complexity of diasporic locations and binational affiliations is often misunderstood in India. The criticism of not being authentic is the ultimate censure served to the diasporic performer. This oversimplified reading of diasporic locations is captured in the experiences of a few second-generation South Asian American performers, mostly in their early twenties, who have gone back to India to establish themselves as musicians. In India, these musicians are often dubbed NRI (non-resident Indian) musicians.[31] There is a definite divide between performers born and raised in India and those from the diaspora (the NRIs). Raghu Kumar, a young tech entrepreneur and a musician, produced regular podcasts and maintained an information database about Carnatic music in the diaspora, in order to "get the music out." He told me during an interview I conducted: "The label NRI sticks even if you try to avoid it. If you are from the diaspora, then music organizers introduce you as from the US or from UK. It's like a quota system for NRIs when it comes to being featured in primetime concerts."

Consider another artist, Sandeep Narayan, who studied Carnatic music from the age of four while growing up in California. After having graduated from the University of California, he has moved to Chennai, India, to pursue a career as a professional classical singer. In the city of Chennai, where I interviewed him, Sandeep mentioned he is labeled as "the guy from America." In an article for the *Hindu*, Sandeep writes:

> The process of trying to be taken seriously as a professional musician has been no cake walk. For starters, the label of being an "NRI" musician is often extremely difficult to shed . . . Explaining that I have moved to Chennai can be tiring at times, but it's something one gets used to and it just furthers the idea that one must live in Chennai to become a serious Carnatic musician.[32]

There are different modes of criticism directed to the diasporic musician: their pronunciation is too American or not authentic enough, or organizers are paying them undue attention just because of their non-resident status. The diaspora, in order to be legitimate in the eyes of the nation, has to demonstrate its authenticity through mimetic performances that can claim both fidelity and allegiance to the original. Or in a Benjaminian sense, they have to be able to capture the elusive aura both in the fidelity of their performance and through their authentic bodily comportment.

As a rich circulatory site inscribed and embedded with contradictions, the diaspora offers an excellent opportunity, according to Radhakrishnan (1996: 213), "to think through some of these vexed questions: solidarity and criticism, belonging and distance, insider spaces and outsider spaces, identity as invention and identity as natural, location-subject positionality and the politics of representation, rootedness and rootlessness." Many of these themes echo in the sensory and affective regimes that connect transnational diasporic communities and nations. This discussion of Carnatic music pedagogy, organized around prescriptive notions of authenticity, troubles the romanticized conceptualization of the diaspora as preoccupied with reproducing the homeland. While to an extent the foundational trope continues to run through the narrative attaching the diaspora, home, and homeland, the connections are established not through older articulations of nostalgia and imaginary homelands, but rather in the form of far more dynamic and participatory encounters enabled by technology. In the context of the global economy, the nation and the diaspora are not discrete or isolable categories (Axel, 2002); instead, they are locked in a relationship underwritten by the global capital, ideologies of authenticity, and technologies of mediation. In his classic formulation about contested diasporic sensibilities, Clifford (1997: 225) writes that diaspora cultures "mediate, in a lived tension, the experiences of separation and entanglement, of living here and remembering/desiring another space." However, in this new global diasporic iteration in the neoliberal context, we see a different narrative emerging. While the contemporary diasporic experience still has the elements of longing, memory, and entanglements, technology and the force of global economy radically rework the transnational experience in terms of a sustained connectivity and synchronicity.

In this chapter, I have mapped the ways in which the authenticity of form and performance is actively imagined by and produced for the diaspora. The rhetoric of authenticity tends to degenerate into essentialized binaries (Radhakrishnan, 1996) and its worth is deeply connected to a materiality of presentation, putative aura, and commodity value. The performative arena described in this chapter shows how the mobilization of the authentic and the process of authentication find a place in the diasporic every day through an assemblage of global actors. This process is repeated through different domains of diasporic social life and activity, and each time authenticity is predicated on the notion of the reproducible original. Once perceived as the remembered recreation of the nation, the diasporic experience is itself transformed as digital cultures reorganize and rescript the sensory landscape of globalization. In the labor of reviving authentic traditions, there is both a heightened awareness of mediation and a belief that technology enables us to transcend the digital interface and enter a post-auratic realm where reproductions seem more authentic than the original. What makes these technologies of connection and transmission interesting is not their wondrous potential to compress, accelerate, and reproduce. Rather, these technologies help us think about the social worlds enabled by the mediated linkages of the diaspora and the nation.

# 7 Conclusion: Destinations and Beginnings

As key moments in the migrant experience, arrivals and departures are often perceived as new beginnings and endings. While these moments stand out as historic markers in individual and collective lives, they are also deeply intertwined from a conceptual, political, and material standpoint. From the perspective of the state, there is a very clear beginning to the linear story of migration and legitimate citizenship. It is only when an immigrant is deemed ready to be naturalized that life as a citizen truly begins. However, from the migrant's perspective, the narration of these beginnings is much more circuitous and tangled. In his profound meditation on method, Said (1975: 13) writes that a beginning is already "a project underway," inaugurating a deliberate production of meaning. This reminder to take circularity into account, and be mindful of points of critical departure, is particularly relevant in our attempts to understand how immigrant trajectories and diasporic publics are constituted. In this final chapter, I take a step back to view and weave together themes raised earlier and offer more descriptive support to the ways in which power structures, identity work, and everyday meanings intersect. The elaborations presented in this section also revisit the need to broaden scholarly contextualization of the global landscapes in which migration and its politics are enacted.

Throughout this book, I have engaged with how the regulation of migrants, systems of representation, and the cultural productions of diasporic communities are shaped within the overlapping space of transnational geographies and shifting media ecologies. Bringing media and migration into the same frame forces a rethinking of systems of inclusion and exclusion and a focus on how, as Kraidy (2013: 4) notes, "power shapes representations, infrastructures and flows in global communication." The chapters cohere around the premise that migration troubles assumptions that sustain singular conceptualizations of community, identity, and linear notions of communication. As many of the examples and instances discussed so far have demonstrated, immigrant sagas have no easy beginnings or endings. However, mapping the perspectives of those who live transnationally throws light on the contradictions and tensions that characterize mobile locations (Ossman, 2007). The mobility of migrants is either shaped or arrested, their presence valorized or ignored, by articulations of power, risk, and the manipulative fluidity of the neoliberal economy. The contestations and cultural practices of transnational communities are a vital part of understanding the diasporic everyday experience. While I have drawn attention to these issues throughout the book, in this concluding chapter I discuss some particular assemblages conjoining market logics, space, and communication practices that frame the experience of mobility and migration. I elaborate on the politics of migration, drawing attention to how lines of power are strategically mobilized in specific sites with regard to (1) the role of documents and the circulation of control; (2) national identity and anxieties over cohesion; (3) space and assertions of ownership; and (4) neoliberal logics and valuation of difference. These interrelated themes reinforce the overarching perspective that migration is a highly charged, multiply mediated, and deeply contested subject whose meanings span transnational domains.

## Document Power

Writing about the centrality of documents to the ways people think as well as to the social order they inhabit, Gitelman (2014: 5) notes: "documents belong to that ubiquitous subcategory of texts that embraces the subjects and instruments of bureaucracy or of systematic knowledge generally." In the modern era, Gitelman (2014) argues, the cultural weight of documents depends on their institutional frames, and bureaucracies not only employ but also are shaped by documents. The excruciating demands and banality of paperwork define the very conditions of migrant existence. At every stage of immigration, there is intense activity concerning documents and paperwork, all of which require negotiation with the power structures and bureaucracies of multiple nations. The gathering, attesting, updating, and renewing of documents is a routine part of migrant life. In diasporic social gatherings, conversation often veers to topics such as visa status, the current wait time for citizenship, and the complexity of forms, permits, and certificates. I have observed this happen in many social situations when South Asians in the United States gather; in all likelihood, the same happens with other immigrant communities as well. Details are shared about the intricate balancing of familial situations and about complicated processes regarding the process of acquiring citizenship or navigating dual citizenships. Functioning with the protocols of governmentality is part of the existential reality that preoccupies transnational communities. While paperwork is necessary to have the freedom to move, the process delivers individuals into the complex apparatus of state control.

The highly mediated front of the state apparatus is, of course, most visible at immigration checkpoints at airports, and at borders worldwide. Visas, passports, and permits do not merely record a preexisting reality, according to McKeown (2011: 2), but rather are "part of a global process of creating stable, documentable identities for individuals, and dividing those individuals across an international system of nation states." The interview at the airport is a classic example of the interrogation and examination that enables the identification of those considered undesirable entrants to the nation. The quick double-take by the agent at the photograph in the passport and the real face in front of the counter seems intended to provoke anxiety. Typically, the agent flips through the passport and scrutinizes visas, work authorization, and permits. At the moment of recognition, the official stamp of approval is registered only for those deemed fit to be welcomed into the nation. The period prior to the moment of arrival is typically one of anxious waiting for paperwork to be processed by immigration authorities. People stand in long lines at consulates and embassy offices where the suitability of visa applicants to be recognized and/or admitted is vetted. The text and inscriptions on the passport emplace personal history in the infrastructure of state surveillance. Kumar (2000: 3) makes an interesting point about the act of reading the passport as a public document and as personal history.

> If we allow that the passport is a kind of book, we might see the immigrant as a very different kind of reader than the officer seated at his desk with a gleaming badge on his uniform. The immigrant's reading of that book refers to an outside world that is more real. The officer is paid to make a connection only between the book and the person standing in front of him.

Historically, the scrutiny of the face and the close reading of the photograph have both been highly racialized and sexualized exercises. An important example is the Page Law of 1875, which barred the entry of undesirable immigrants. Chinese women who emigrated at that time were subject to a humiliating practice of cross-checking photographs in order to visually assess if they were wives or prostitutes. Photographs that had been sent in advance to immigration officials were compared to the ones brought by the women on arrival. Tracing the history of exclusionary control at the US border, Luibhéid (2002) notes that Chinese women were the first group of immigrants whose mobility was regulated by the exchange of photographs between officials, based on the assumption that the bodies and demeanor of prostitutes were visibly and recognizably distinct. With the overlaying of biographical information on the photographic image, a case file was created that constituted a group of people, in Foucault's (1977: 190) words, as "a describable, analyzable object."[1]

The citizenship tests are another site of paper and power in the immigration process. Designed mainly in the late nineteenth century to discourage specific groups of people from entering, the current tests are becoming sophisticated technologies of disciplinary power. They now assume standardized formats that test knowledge of the political process and at the same time attempt to assess values and the potential for civic integration (Löwenheim and Gazit, 2009). Some of the newer tests seem to be designed with the view of curbing the number of Muslim immigrants to Europe. For example, in 2005, the Dutch government created a two-hour film that included scenes of a woman sunbathing topless, and another scene of two men kissing in a meadow. The rationale behind this film, according to immigration officials, was to expose potential immigrants to the liberal values and the way life is lived in the Netherlands.[2] However, what this reinstates is the unquestioned sexual modernity of the West and the presumption of the unassimilability of migrants from Muslim countries. The arguments are very similar to the ones mobilized in opposition to the veil, discussed earlier in chapter 4. In this case, alternative sexualities are used to signify the nation's liberal values (a tenuous assumption at best),[3] and the test seems intentionally designed to act as a strategic tactic intended to shock and hence filter immigrants. Citizenship tests reveal the state's stance of suspicion about immigrants, and according to Löwenheim and Gazit (2009: 161) are "telling of a new conception of citizenship, in which the state claims a right to probe the inner/emotional worlds of immigrants." The use of documents and testing creates classifications that separate and stratify publics. The desperation for authorization and economic necessity drive immigrants to find innovative ways of overcoming these demands of the state by working the brisk informal economy of counterfeit paperwork. Undocumented and irregular immigrants often become dependent on criminal networks for paperwork in order to survive. Vasta (2010: 189) makes the insightful point that as immigrants find ways to deal with or circumvent regulations, they often "construct flexible and innovative identities, though not in circumstances of their choosing."

In a dramatic scene in Adichie's (2013) novel *Americanah*, a British National Insurance number, an indispensable form of identification in the UK, is traded in a London flat. The exchange transforms the identity of one of the central characters, Obinze, the son of a college professor in Nigeria. Now as an irregular migrant in the UK in need of papers, Obinze buys the prized identification number, thereby becoming Vincent, born in Birmingham. The number, a piece of information, a requirement of the state, totally subsumes Obinze. Through the power and the magic of that number, he emerges as Vincent, his new global avatar. With this new possession, his whole persona changes and so too his social network and the possibilities of holding a job in the UK. As Vincent, Obinze has an identity recognized by the state; he can now work and open a bank account. For this rented identity, Obinze is expected to pay 40 percent of what he earns. Life is not always predictable or safe when one lives precariously balancing a fake identity. When a little boy in a café asks Obinze if he lives in London, it sets off a ripple of existential anxiety that Adichie captures with deep insight:

> Yes, Obinze said, but that yes did not tell his story, that he lived in London indeed but invisibly, his existence like an erased pencil sketch; each time he saw a policeman, or anyone in a uniform, anyone with the faintest scent of authority, he would fight the urge to run. (Adichie, 2013: loc. 4358)

Narratives of migrant life develop within and around paperwork, the power of information, and the fluid exigencies of transnational lives. The migratory journey has deep-rooted beginnings and distant endings that are public and private, personal and structural, hidden and visible, at the same time. The perspective of the state, however, hinges on an anachronistic linear narrative and the production of the immigrant as the outsider, as clearly seen in the excruciating logics of the paperwork described. This imaginary of a singular community that continues to exert a strong influence in spite of the growing heterogeneity of populations is described by Amin (2012: loc. 127) as "regressive for its veiled xenophobia and exclusionary nostalgia, and unrealistic for its denial of the plural constituency of modern being and belonging." In the next section, I engage with how this denial and anxieties about the national imaginary are reproduced and exacerbated by representational logics.

## Other Anxieties

The media both reflect and take their cue from the logic of the security state and its effort to produce the singular national body through elaborate forms of surveillance and policing. Today, militarized and technologized borders represent the material sites where nations assert their sovereign power and where hegemonic forms of citizenship are normalized.[4] Undesirable bodies are identified and marked through the use of various technologies of surveillance and interrogation. Classification, in the manner described by Foucault (1977: 191), recreates individuals as cases where they are "described, judged, measured, compared with others." Immigration is a classic site where individuals are scrutinized and defined as cases, types, and numbers. The ambivalent relationship between the nation and the immigrant, according to Behdad (2005: 172), "makes us understand the productive function of the immigrant, whose perennial figuration as a threatening other in the democratic imaginary has perpetually helped to fashion an exclusionary sense of belonging and also to entrench and rationalize the state's disciplinary power over its citizens."

In Hamid's 2007 novel *The Reluctant Fundamentalist*, there is a telling scene that takes place at the airport in New York. The protagonist, the successful, Ivy-League-educated Pakistani Changez, is returning to New York from a business trip with his colleagues, soon after September 11, 2001.

> When we arrived, I was separated from my team at immigration. They joined the queue for American citizens; I joined the one for foreigners. The officer who inspected my passport was a solidly built woman with a pistol at her hip and a mastery of English inferior to mine; I attempted to disarm her with a smile. "What is the purpose of your trip to the United States?" she asked me. "I live here," I replied. "That is not what I asked you, sir," she said. "What is the purpose of your trip to the United States?" Our exchange continued in much this fashion for several minutes. In the end I was dispatched for a secondary inspection in a room where I sat on a metal bench next to a tattooed man in handcuffs. My team did not wait for me; by the time I entered the customs hall they had already collected their suitcases and left. As a consequence, I rode to Manhattan very much alone. (Hamid, 2007: 75)

This passage captures the way in which certain immigrants are being perceived as bodies of risk and danger to the nation in the aftermath of the September 11 attacks in the United States. The circularity of the interchange between Changez and the immigration officer is another revealing instance of the reading of the passport. While Changez' presence and response rest on a complex combination of factors such as his status, accomplishments, postcolonial class background, and superior mastery of the English language, the immigration agent sees him, first and foremost, as a prototype of risk. The element of suspicion about the Other, and more specifically about Muslims, has become part of the everyday culture of the security state. As Cacho (2012: 98) writes, the terrorist becomes a composite figure built on existing dangers, and this "new enemy" is "juridically, discursively and relationally produced during the war on terror." The media, in turn, ratchet up fear about the presence of dangerous Others, thereby setting them apart from the national community. These fears of menacing foreign bodies have penetrated into the banal rhythms of social life and are enacted both on the street and on the screen. Immigrants with and without papers and even naturalized citizens of certain racial backgrounds are all rendered suspect and subject to scrutiny. The backlash against Muslims in the West has been intense,[5] as some of the discussion in the earlier part of this book revealed.

Pain and Smith (2008: 2) argue for the importance of bringing together the geopolitical and the everyday aspects of fear in order to understand how global insecurities and instabilities work their way into local landscapes of risk. We need to include the media in all its forms and practices into this constellation of factors, in order to grapple with the complexities of migration and migrant identities.

This fear of the Other is not new, and the racial composition of a changing nation has been a cause of great anxiety at various points in history. For example, stories about new "waves" and "floods" of immigrant populations and predictions about the time when whites will become a minority, or when Europe will be transformed into Eurabia, have become media staples. In the United States, a flurry of news reports usually follow the census numbers that show the "browning" of America, or how Americans identify themselves along racial lines or not. Over the years, *Time* magazine covers on immigrants are a case in point. In 1985, *Time* magazine ran a special issue with the caption, "Immigrants: The Changing face of America." The cover showed a lineup of profiles from different racial backgrounds, mostly non-white, looking away from the reader, evoking the memory of Ellis Island. The faces are serious and look away in anticipation at a life that is yet to unfold. The text makes reference to the ways in which the waves of immigration are transforming the nation: "They come from everywhere, for all kinds of reasons, and they are rapidly and permanently changing the face of America."[6] While there is an enthusiastic emphasis on the vitality and energy of immigrants, there is also the implication that something is slipping away – the homogenous racial face of the nation.

Five years later in another issue on the demographics of the nation, the text on the cover of *Time* magazine (April 9, 1990) was much more direct: "America's Changing Colors: What Will the U.S. Be Like When Whites Are No Longer the Majority?" On the cover is the picture of the American flag with black, brown, and yellow filling out the areas that were previously white. The white areas of the flag peek out at the edges, while interestingly the yellow stripe is the most prominent. As one of the articles in the magazine states: "The deeper significance of America becoming a majority non-white society is what it means to the national psyche, to individuals' sense of themselves and the nation – their idea of what it is to be American."[7] Asian Americans, despite their smaller numbers compared to Latinos, are represented as the main economic threat. This cover, according to Leo Chavez (2001), suggests that Asian Americans exert an influence that goes beyond their numbers, implying that the greater threat comes from the economic strength that Asian American communities exert in the nation rather than from demographic strength. In addition, the cover image and text within seem to suggest that with demographic changes, the nation and the idea of who is considered "American" will be radically changed.

The 1993 immigration cover of *Time* magazine featured the caption: "The New Face of America: How Immigrants Are Shaping the World's First Multicultural Society" (November 18, 1993). This time around the cover carried a computer-generated image – a female face representing, according to the accompanying text, a composite of Anglo-Saxon, Middle Eastern, African, Asian, Hispanic, and Southern European features. In contrast to the earlier covers, this one moves away from the huddled masses lineup to a face of an imagined woman, an individual standing in for many others. In an astute analysis, Berlant (1997) makes the point that the first *Time* magazine cover in 1985 captured the unfolding history of immigrants as one that is yet to be made; a history that is conflated with the fact of emerging as new citizens. In 1993, the immigrant becomes an imagined body, a digital rendering delinked from any material collective or community, devoid of agency, and "stands in pure isolation from lived history" (Berlant 1997: 177).

In 2012, once again, *Time* magazine ran an issue on the immigration story, with the caption: "We Are Americans: Just Not Legally." The cover featured journalist Jose Antonio Vargas, the celebrated undocumented immigrant discussed in chapter 2, along with other young undocumented immigrants. The caption carried the words from the article written by Vargas in the issue: "We're some of the nearly 12 million undocumented immigrants living in the U.S. Why we're done hiding." While the group featured on the magazine's cover in 1985 looked away from the reader, this group of young people looks directly at the reader with deep intensity and seriousness. A backstory on the making of the issue states that it was important for *Time*'s photo editors to show just how many cultures are represented by America's undocumented immigrants. According to Gian Paul Lozza, who photographed the cover: "We wanted to bring that diversity to the light. This is not just a problem for Latinos as we hear about often, but for every culture from around the world."[8] In a promotional video about the making of the 2012 cover, the group is lined up as if in a naturalization ceremony and they talk about their lofty aspirations and goals.[9] The cover presents the young Dreamers as achievers and doers who lack papers but are ready to communicate and publicize their cause in the media.

These various covers of the magazine capture the national imaginary over time about migrants in our midst. The visuals move from the celebration of the immigrant as an American in the making, to the digital representation of the immigrant as composite, and finally to the immigrant as the aspirational subject. All the images are consistent in their downplaying of the history, politics, and particularity of migration narratives. Instead what is reproduced is the image of immigrants as stereotypical streams of cultural Others entering the sanctity of the national space.

The recurrent reconfiguration of patterns of national anxiety over race and immigration is related to the long histories of resistance to the presence of immigrants. The most recent iteration is the extreme reactions to the presence of Muslim immigrants in the West, as discussed in earlier chapters. Several scholars have considered at length how each wave of immigrants has been met by different scripts of racialized resentment and resistance from local citizens.[10] As these reactions now circulate and gain new forms of visibility on mediated platforms, negative affect and everyday policing toward new publics are routinized. As Appadurai (2006: 84) states, "minorities in a globalizing world are a constant reminder of the incompleteness of national purity." To dominant groups, minoritized spaces, to which I turn next, serve as visible markers of a lost homogeneity.

## Space Claims

Global cities are connected transnationally through both formal and informal circuits of capital. While hegemonic scripts of globalization privilege processes and actors that support the flow of corporate capital (Sassen, 1998), ethnic spaces offer a counter-narrative. Urban diasporation has created vibrant market spaces that are supported by alternative, and sometimes hidden, flows of capital and goods. Catering both to the immigrant community and beyond, these ethnic and minoritized spaces evoke the sensory textures and densities of faraway places and are emblematic of greater demographic transformations. While they stand out as islands of difference, their very presence also globalizes the city and produces the cosmopolitanism of urban life. The spatial practices of transnational communities are in fact claims for legitimacy and assertions of group identities.

To diasporic communities who balance their lives transnationally, the categories of the global and local are very fluid and reflect the complex sets of material realities that frame their everyday experiences. Spaces gain meaning in response to these shifting expectations. In ethnic spaces, we see mimetic processes at work where active recreations and reproductions of cultural practices take place as migrants reimagine their lives. Mandel (2008), in her rich ethnography of Turkish immigrants in the Kreuzberg area of Berlin, makes a provocative argument about the ethnicization of space. While Turks in their own native environment are considered by the West as exotic, once in the West their faith and sartorial and food choices are considered simply too foreign. Hence, as Mandel (2008: 142) argues, "Kreuzberg has been caught between German fears of, first, the foreigner, overforeignization and, second, the desire to share in the creativity of minor cultures." So alternately migrants and their spaces shift in the dominant imaginary from fear and resentment to curiosity and desire. Now in an ironical twist, areas of global cities, like New York's Chinatown or London's East End, that were once regarded as immigrant neighborhoods are slowly being reinvented as trendy, alternative places as a result of gentrification.

Migrants themselves contribute to the tourist economy and add to the overall attraction of the global city for visitors. The image of migrants typically from the Global South selling T-shirts, watches, and purses has become a familiar sight of street-side commerce in major cities of the West. In addition, ethnic areas of the city are also promoted as spaces of consumption and tourism in the global city. A tour of ethnic neighborhoods, like Kreuzberg in Berlin or Jackson Heights in New York, is routinely suggested in tourist itineraries as an authentic ethnic experience that completes any visit to the global city. The cultures of these transnational communities are essentialized and commodified as attractions, transforming the gritty materialities of migration into palatable, apolitical narratives, ready-made for touristic consumption. The discourse of tourism contains the ethnic community within the enclosure of the minoritized space. In this way diasporic cultures can be safely consumed and the overall experience lends global cachet to the city.[11]

To migrant communities, these spaces have social and political significance. Strategically positioned both for community support and for commerce, they have typically grown through careful networking and collective action. Diasporic spaces grow over time and sustain immigrant communities, making available the commodities, flavors, and support services to reproduce lifestyles and other familiar routines of everyday life. But in the eyes of many, these spaces are intrusive and out of place. For example, in 2009, a clear majority supported a ban on the construction of minarets in Switzerland as a way of containing the perceived Islamization of the country and notably its skyline.[12] In 2010, resistance to building an Islamic cultural center in downtown Manhattan, also fueled by the media, stirred a national controversy; other mosque projects around the United States have met with similar opposition.[13] These forms of resistance are not isolated eruptions or racist outbursts, but rather represent a recurring pattern by which ideologies concerning the nation and its rightful citizens are reproduced. For instance, in October 2002, in a response to what was perceived as a Somali invasion, the mayor of Lewiston in Maine wrote an open letter to the community leaders in the Somali refugee community who had relocated to Maine. In his highly dramatic and publicized letter, the mayor stated: "Our city is maxed out financially, physically and emotionally" (Finnegan, 2006: 48). He then implored the Somalis to ease the flow and stop bringing their friends and families to Lewiston. Rumors were spreading that the Somalis would bankrupt the town. The mayor's letter became a national and international story, even inciting a white supremacist group to organize a rally in Lewiston.[14] It was the writing of the letter, a rather strange and arrogant mediated enactment of presumed civility, that constituted the tipping point. The Somali presence is inserted into a well-rehearsed narrative of contamination, supported within an established dominant version of national identity. In his analysis of immigration in the European context, Balibar (1991: 7) makes the claim that "before there can be any serious analysis of racism and its relationship to migrations, we have to ask ourselves what this word 'Europe' means and what it will signify tomorrow." Racism, according to Balibar's argument, is never really just about the relationship to the Other, but is a relationship that is defined and mediated by state intervention. To this equation that connects the state, racism, and the Other, we should add the role of media and technology in intensifying the negative affect and facilitating the strategic insertion of market-driven dynamics into the immigration domain.

## Neoliberal Logics

In September 2014, in an unprecedented event in New York City, a large gathering of Indian Americans filled the arena at Madison Square Garden to welcome the prime minister of India, Narendra Modi, on his first state visit to the United States. The diaspora gave a rousing rock-star welcome, complete with the energetic beat of Bollywood music, to the head of state from the homeland. Red, white, and blue balloons filled the arena and rose up to the ceiling together with green, saffron, and white balloons, representing the colors of both the American and the Indian flags. The stage was crowded with US lawmakers, and the national anthems of the two countries were sung with much fanfare. Making a sensational entrance, Prime Minister Modi's address reached out to the diaspora's pride in their homeland by declaring that this was not only the Asian century, but also the Indian century. He appealed to the diaspora to serve "Mother India" and even promised to simplify immigration processes for naturalized US citizens to get lifetime visas and stay connected with the homeland.[15]

This event signifies some very important turns in how diasporas are being redefined and their connections to the homeland rearticulated in the context of globalization and its economic imperatives. Prime Minister Modi was reaching out to a largely professional, middle-class diasporic base in the United States who already have strong cultural, political, and financial ties with India. It was a clear and direct appeal to the economic power and investment potential of the Indian American diaspora. Prime Minister Modi's speech was not urging the diaspora to return but rather was enabling, or leveraging, their cosmopolitan status as global Indians. The social media publicity and this rousing media blitz was a definitive moment that changed the discourse of national expectations with regard to the diaspora. In an interview about the event, Rajagopal (2014) offers the compelling explanation that Modi's reaching out to global Indians was a way of saying:

> We are proud of the Indian diaspora, keep doing what you are doing, keep supporting us in the ways that you are supporting us, but we don't demand that you come back to the homeland, in order to really belong. So that old guilt trip which emigrants have always wrestled with is now definitively over, and that too from the most nationalist prime minister we have ever had.

Prime Minister Modi's strategic reaching out and appeal to the South Asian diaspora captures the nation's investment in the global identity and flexible affiliations of its diaspora as a way of securing India's own global image. As privileged global citizens, the diaspora is celebrated as integrally connected rather than removed from the homeland. Since the New York visit, it is telling that Prime Minister Modi has met with the Indian diaspora in several other countries. The nation relies on select members of its diaspora to create and circulate a signature global brand. The rhetoric, propped and amplified by a media apparatus, reinscribes the diaspora within the nation in a revised form of long-distance nationalism.[16]

Under neoliberalism, the logics of the marketplace have been firmly inserted into the realm of national politics and citizenship. According to Ong (2006: 6), the "elements that we think of as coming together to create citizenship – rights, entitlements, territoriality, a nation – are becoming disarticulated and rearticulated with forces set into motion by market forces." The previous example about Indian Americans highlights the privileging of a certain type of economic migrant – the entrepreneurial diasporic subject favored on both sides of the migration itinerary. However, global capital flows and neoliberal economic transformations also necessitate other types of classed mobility, and all these various trajectories are entangled in complex formations. Neoliberal global economic policies have ushered in the slow devaluation of the public sector, a steady emphasis on privatization, the growth of the service industry, the prioritization of an ethos of individualism, and a reliance on a flexible and disposable workforce. The devastating global implications of these changes has led to profound inequities and, consequently, the emergence of a vast and vulnerable migrant precariat: a population regarded by Bauman (2003: 57) as "the flotsam and jetsam of the planetary tides of human waste." Describing this shadow reserve army, Standing (2011: 90) writes: "Migrants make up a large share of the world's precariat. They are a cause of its growth and in danger of becoming its primary victims, demonized and made the scapegoat of problems not of their making. Yet, with few exceptions, all they are doing is trying to improve their lives." The individual desires and aspirations of migrants are necessarily entrapped within much larger global narratives of supply and demand for a disposable workforce.

In recent years in the United States, the rate of deportation of young undocumented migrants to countries including, among others, Mexico, Guatemala, Honduras, and the Dominican Republic have been at an all-time high.[17] Most of the deported migrants belong to the generation of the Dreamers (described earlier in the book), who were brought to the United States as young children and raised without documents or status. Now, as they are being deported to the countries they barely know or understand, their fluency in American English makes them suddenly attractive as flexible labor for global capital. Call centers are springing up in Mexico and Guatemala where young deportees are hired to speak fluent American English to customers in a variety of services. Handling calls for US companies, they are talking to customers about warranties, returns, parcel deliveries, and other service-related issues. Deportees have the added advantage of being able to engage in small talk and chitchat with customers about sports and everyday life in the United States. In the early 2000s, call centers gravitated to India, due to the country's colonial history and the presence of a vast pool of English-speaking workers. However, the recruits in India had to be trained by corporations to imitate accents familiar to the customers in the West. In an ironic twist and contrast, the deportees are ready-made American employees who can be paid at lower rates, because they are not Americans, yet American enough to function for the economy. To the previously undocumented and now deported call-center workers in Mexico and Guatemala, the job is welcome, as it provides employment while in a country that is deemed their home, but one they barely know. Ironically, the job and its language requirements trigger some level of affective connection with a lifestyle associated with their past and socialization in the US. The parents of these deportees were forced out of their countries due to the dire circumstances created in the developing world by the global economy. Now, in this next iteration of global capitalism, the traumas of immigration and deportation are rescripted with the help of technology, to serve the interests of transnational corporations and their need for flexible labor.[18]

These two scenarios concerning two different immigration contexts reveal the complex connections between nationalism, capitalism, immigration, and labor. This nexus also frames the changing conditions under which migrant subjectivities are represented, performed, and made relevant under the logics of the marketplace. With media technologies enabling time/space compressions, globalization has a way of finding value in every crevice of opportunity. The neoliberal economy finds multiple ways of creating market opportunities out of the longings, desire, and attachments of migrants. High-speed communication, media technologies, and the compression of space-time dimensions make these forms of neoliberal valuations and global opportunities possible. Whether it is selling *hijabs* online to the diaspora,[19] arranging for burials in the home country, offering wedding packages in the homeland, selling mobiles, enabling remittances, or a host of other services for migrants, market logics successfully commodify and create value out of migrant lives, affect, longings, and attachments. Migrants too use and rely on the shifting patterns of the economy to find their place in the world. The logics of the neoliberal economy intertwine with media and communication systems to play a contextual and instrumental role in the articulation of cultural citizenship.

Destinations in the migrant imaginary are distant end goals but also ones that dynamically drive and represent beginnings, whether existential, material, or aspirational. The explorations in this book have also been mindful of this sense of multiple beginnings and endings in order to loosen fixities and think about migration and media in nuanced ways. The chapters of this book have wrestled at various levels with aspects of the questions listed here: How do migrants perform and re/produce their transnational locations? How are fields of meaning created, enabled, circumscribed, and experienced? How do we describe the experience of transnational mobility and its intersections with complex lines of power? Why and how do we arrive at or begin from particular types of material and discursive sites and formations? What are the circuitous trajectories through which ideas and ideologies concerning migration come to visibility? How do nations and publics connect and authenticate their presence? How are identities and cultures performed and mediated via digital pathways? The intersection of migration and media presents both a challenge and an opportunity to track the ways in which social issues extend beyond and across national boundaries. Across disciplines, the current challenge of globalization has been to find creative ways of understanding the problematics of circulation, connectivity, and mobility and the transformations they engender. These realities come together, especially around the subject of migration, as unforeseen configurations or familiar rearrangements shaped and scripted by the mediascapes and media cultures of globalization.

Collectively, the chapters in this book attempt to capture the unevenness of the global terrain by paying attention to how the subject of migration is inserted into local, national, and transnational imaginaries and regimes of being. Localities, according to Appadurai (2010), where "our vitally important archives reside" are not "subordinate instances of the global, but in fact the main evidence of its reality." As we have seen in this book, discussions of difference, volatile eruptions over the presence of immigrants, and the panic they stir in specific communities are all instantiations of a much larger global narrative. The mythology of a coherent and homogenous nation falls apart when we consider the everyday cultures of these transnational communities. Yet firmly held beliefs about belonging and assimilation are enabled and resurrected easily by media technologies, as many of the examples discussed have shown. Even the sights, sounds, and smells of difference are variously deemed intrusive to a sensory balance that is deemed normative to the nation. At the same time, as described earlier, many of these issues are co-opted and reworked as market opportunities in the global economy, supported by the infrastructures of global media and technology.

A defining issue on the global agenda today, immigration will continue to be a contested and controversial subject. There is a steady stream of news almost every day about the flow of migrants and their pathways of travel, shaped by political tensions and economic crises in various parts of the world. Each news story about migration is a provocation to think inclusively about the new publics of globalization. As I wrote this conclusion, a group of writers had registered their anger over the decision of PEN America, a group devoted to preserving freedom of expression, to award the annual Freedom of Expression Courage award to the French satirical magazine *Charlie Hebdo*. Early in 2015, three gunmen opened fire at the Paris headquarters of the magazine, killing 12 people. The magazine's office had been attacked previously, in 2011, after the publication of an issue that featured a caricature of the prophet Mohammed on its cover.[20] While condemning the violence and the brutal attack on the journalists, about 200 members of PEN – including Francine Prose, Teju Cole, Joyce Carol Oates, Peter Carey, Junot Díaz, Lorrie Moore, Michael Ondaatje, and Michael Cunningham – signed a letter of protest at PEN's decision to reward the magazine's controversial cartoon.[21] The writers argued that to "a section of the French population that is already marginalized, embattled and victimized," *Charlie Hebdo*'s satire must be perceived as intending to cause humiliation.

> In the aftermath of the attacks, *Charlie Hebdo*'s cartoons were characterized as satire and "equal opportunity offense," and the magazine seems to be entirely sincere in its anarchic expressions of disdain toward organized religion. But in an unequal society, equal opportunity offense does not have an equal effect.
>
> Power and prestige are elements that must be recognized in considering almost any form of discourse, including satire.[22]

Many writers, including Salman Rushdie, were quick to call the protest misdirected. The letter sparked immediate controversy and an impassioned global exchange that traveled extensively on social media. Upholding *Charlie Hebdo*'s satirical vision, one side applauded the award that recognizes the magazine's courage. The other protesting side, while unequivocally condemning the violence, made a strong argument about the magazine's cultural intolerance, the power of those who can wield discourse, the status of minorities, and the historical legacies that continue to shape social and political connections between peoples. In an interview with the *Guardian*, one of the protesting writers, Amitava Kumar, described the letter as "an appeal for a small pause." "Before we begin clapping, let's ask if we aren't just clapping for ourselves."[23] The protest is a reminder to interrupt the singular narrative of the West and think beyond binary notions of culture, community, and discourse. What are the structures we are upholding and how are we reinforcing them? This returns us directly to some key concerns that migration poses – ones that have been central to this book: What do absolute visions and inflexible assumptions mean and do in a society composed of diverse and deeply divided publics? What sensibilities do we project and what normative structures do they rest on? How do we narrate and make sense of these tensions within the media cultures of globalization? The answers neither are easy nor should be straightforward.

As stated at the outset, my goal was not to focus exclusively on the many technological artifacts, platforms, and devices that constitute the marvel and salve of our interactive times. Rather it was to address how various practices and modalities of communication bridge the representation, experience, and politics of migration. Using the political volatilities and social developments of recent times as a point of departure, I have tried to situate the subject of migration in the context of national logics and mediated fields of meaning that profoundly influence our social worlds. Each of the chapters also explores themes that intersect with and test the limits of concepts that underwrite our understanding of media and communication. If anything, migration pushes us to think transnationally and perhaps question and trouble the methodological nationalism that permeates our understanding of media and migration.[24] The discussions in this book mark connections, note elisions, and track circulatory paths and histories in order to show that migration is not always about flow and mobility but also about various forms of stasis and immobility and about resistance and creativity. The critical challenge is, therefore, not to tell a singular story with a defined beginning and end but to disrupt the power of the linear narrative. *Mediating Migration* is an effort to capture the multiplicity of meanings, connections, and collisions that define the politics of global mobility.

# Notes

## Chapter 1 Introduction

1  Semple, 2008.
2  On the role of letters in the migration experience see Elliott, Gerber, and Sinke, 2006.
3  Advancing a strong case, Ong (1999: 4) argues that the *trans* in transnationality suggests both movement and change: "Besides suggesting new relations between nation-states and capital, transnationality also alludes to the *trans*versal, the *trans*actional, the *trans*lational, and the *trans*gressive aspects of contemporary behavior and imagination that are incited, enabled, and regulated by the changing logics of states and capitalism." This critical move is very useful in conceptualizing and tracking the social, political, and economic circuits of migration.
4  Appadurai (2006: 28) writes that cellular forms of organization are "connected yet not vertically managed, coordinated yet remarkably independent, capable of replication without central messaging structures, hazy in their central organizational features yet crystal clear in their cellular strategies and effects." He argues that terrorist networks and their forms of decentralized organizing exemplify this cellular mode of organizing. Non-state organizations, according to Appadurai (2006), committed to goals of equity also subscribe to these proliferating forms of cellularity.
5  The neoliberal global economy with policies such as the North American Free Trade Agreement, the growth of the service economy, and the feminization of work have profoundly impacted the flow of migrants in recent times. For a detailed overview of global migration and histories, see, for example, Castles, de Haas, and Miller, 2013; Zolberg, 2006; Brettell and Hollifield, 2000; Papastergiadis, 2000.
6  Preston, 2010.
7  Lacey, 2010.
8  Gammeltoft-Hansen, 2012.
9  Belluck, 2000.
10  https://prelectur.stanford.edu/lecturers/robinson/inaugural.html.
11  http://www.uscis.gov/us-citizenship/naturalization-test/naturalization-oath-allegiance-united-states-america.
12  All quotations from Stanmeyer can be found at Stanmeyer, 2014.
13  The work on ethnic cultural production and journalistic representation of immigration is too vast to review here. Significant examples include: King

and Wood, 2001; Chavez, L., 2001, 2013; McKinnon, 2009; Orgad, 2012; Benson, 2013.

14 See, for example, Punathambekar, 2005; Moorti, 2007; Valdivia, 2010; Echchaibi, 1999, 2011.

15 http://venturebeat.com/2011/03/17/u-s-immigrant-smartphone-owners-drive-video-calls.

16 This point was made to me in a passing conversation I had with some South Asian construction workers in Abu Dhabi. The careful selection of sites that are photographed by migrants is also documented by Gardner, 2012.

17 For an analysis of the portrayal of the everyday in immigrant lives, see Dyer, 2002.

18 On the concept of mediation in media studies, see Silverstone, 2005; Livingstone, 2009; Deuze, 2012.

19 Martinez, Yan, and Shoichet, 2014.

20 Douglas, 1978.

21 Nyers, 2008.

22 Freedman, 2012.

### Chapter 2 Legitimacy: Accumulating Status

1 Dembour and Kelly, 2011; Koopmans, Statham, Giugni, and Passy, 2005.

2 Bogado, 2013.

3 The rally was organized by the New York State Youth Leadership Council to push for federal action and a fair path to citizenship. The term "Dreamers" is used to refer to undocumented youth and comes from the DREAM Act, an acronym for Development, Relief, and Education for Alien Minors, a legislative proposal that was originally introduced in 2001.

4 Bada, Fox, and Selee, 2006.

5 This number, 11.4 million, is from 2012 and can be found in Baker and Rytina, 2013.

6 On the subject of undocumented migrants mobilizing for rights in France, Canada, Italy, and the UK see Nyers, 2003; McNevin, 2006; Oliveri, 2012; Nair, 2012; Marciniak and Tyler, 2014.

7 Jayal (2013) on thin and thick conceptualizations and their assumed sequestration has been very helpful here. The notion of citizenship-as-status versus citizenship-as-activity is also discussed by Kymlicka and Norman, 1994.

8 For more work on the protests of the undocumented, see Nyers, 2010; Rigby and Schlembach, 2013.

9 Beamon and Bachman, 2013.

10 Le, 2013.

11 Vargas, 2013c.

12 Krikorian, 2013.

13 Vargas, 2013b.

14 Vargas, 2013a.

15 On this point, see McNevin, 2007; Tyler and Marciniak, 2013.

16 See, for example, Vargas, 2012c.
17 Remarks by the President on Immigration. http://www.whitehouse.gov/the-press-office/2012/06/15/remarks-president-immigration.
18 See comments in Vargas, 2011.
19 While there are several collections and websites that present the stories of the undocumented, I have mainly focused on David Guggenheim's documentary and website *The Dream Is Now* (http://www.thedreamisnow.org/documentary); Jose Antonio Vargas' site Define American (http://www.defineamerican.com); the *Papers* documentary project (Galisky, 2009) and accompanying book (Manuel, Pineda, Galisky, and Shine, 2012).
20 http://www.thedreamisnow.org/documentary.
21 On this point see Caminero-Santangelo, 2012.
22 Durbin, 2011.
23 In her insightful reading of how wider political discussions on the DREAM Act work their way into local imaginings, Orgad (2012: 115) writes: "These local imaginings do not simply mirror the meta-narrative; they give way to particular readings and articulations of the 'dream' and its meanings."
24 http://www.defineamerican.com/page/about/the-pledge.
25 http://www.change.org/organizations/jose_antonio_vargas_and_define_american.
26 https://www.facebook.com/erika.andiola/posts/4221281926137.
27 http://www.reddit.com/r/IAmA/comments/1eurju.
28 On the subject of coalitional politics see Chavez, K. R., 2013; Morrissey, 2013.
29 Lopez, 2013.
30 At the time of writing, at the tail end of the Obama presidency, the DREAM Act is still tied in a legislative battle embroiled in ideological debates at both local and federal levels.

## Chapter 3  Recognition: Politics and Technologies
1 http://new.mta.info/news/2010/05/03/if-you-see-something-say-something.
2 Kilgannon and Schmidt, 2010.
3 See ch. 5 in Zylinska's (2005) insightful work on the biopolitics of immigration.
4 Thacker, 2005.
5 Fuchs, 2013.
6 Reitman, 2013.
7 Crouch, 2013.
8 Crouch, 2013.
9 http://2001-2009.state.gov/s/ct/rls/rm/2001/5316.htm.
10 Kang, 2013.
11 Kang, 2013.
12 Kang, 2013.
13 Malinowski, 2013.
14 Kang, 2013.

15 Anonymous, 2013.
16 Russert, 2013.
17 Popular stories on Reddit are upvoted and earn points, popularly known as karma points.
18 Greenfield, 2013.
19 Buzzfeed and others who posted inaccurate statements on Twitter have refused to apologize.
20 Fung and Mirkinson, 2013.
21 *Huff Post*, 2013.
22 I draw this notion of the sharing subject from Payne (2013: 554), who argues that the idea of sharing has been fetishized in the context of media virality and the neoliberal economy.
23 For an account of community policing and social media during the Boston bombing, see Keller, 2013; Bar-tur, 2013.
24 See also an interview with Rancière in Rancière and Lie, 2006.
25 Suebsaeng, 2013.
26 http://www.reddit.com/user/bedhead1.
27 For comments, see http://www.reddit.com/user/bedhead1.
28 Brown, 2010.
29 Mesa, 2002.
30 Freedman, 2012.
31 Chen, 2013.
32 In Pictures: Menezes Footage. http://news.bbc.co.uk/2/hi/in_pictures/7038430.stm.
33 Sturcke, 2008.
34 Tomlinson, 2013.
35 On de Menezes' death, also see Vaughan-Williams (2007), where the author refuses to accept that the police shooting was simply a one-off incident that can be isolated from broader aspects of political practice.
36 I draw on Appadurai's (2006) notion of cellularity. This has also been discussed in the Introduction of this book.
37 Highlights of AP's Pulitzer Prize-Winning Probe into NYPD Intelligence Operations. http://www.ap.org/media-center/nypd/investigation.
38 Highlights of AP's Pulitzer Prize-Winning Probe into NYPD Intelligence Operations. http://www.ap.org/media-center/nypd/investigation.
39 Apuzzo and Goldman, 2011.
40 If You See Something, Say Something. http://www.dhs.gov/if-you-see-something-say-something%E2%84%A2.

## Chapter 4  Publics: Eyeing Gender

1 Cowell, 2006b.
2 Radio France International, 2014.
3 Straw, 2006.
4 Johnston, 2006.

5  Straw, 2006.
6  Straw, 2006.
7  Straw, 2006.
8  Straw, 2006.
9  Straw, 2006.
10  BBC News, 2006c.
11  BBC News, 2006.
12  Cowell, 2006a.
13  Cowell, 2006a.
14  Blair, 2006.
15  Blair, 2006.
16  Blair, 2006.
17  Blair, 2006.
18  Kundnani, 2014.
19  Johnston, 2006.
20  After the US invasion of Afghanistan, Laura Bush, in a radio address, stated that "the fight against terrorism is also a fight for the rights and dignity of women" and that "the brutal oppression of women is the central goal of all terrorists." For the text of her address, see: http://www.washingtonpost.com/wp-srv/nation/specials/attacked/transcripts/laurabushtext_111701.html.
21  I draw this notion of intelligibility from Berlant and Warner, 1998: 187.
22  Straw, 2006.
23  Straw, 2006.
24  Straw, 2006.
25  The term was used by David Davis, a conservative MP. See BBC News, 2006b.
26  Straw, 2006.
27  Blair, 2006.
28  See also Riley, 2000.
29  Benahbib, 2002.
30  Straw, 2006.
31  BBC News, 2006a.

## Chapter 5  Domesticity: Digital Visions and Versions

1  On the notion of circulation, I draw on Gaonkar and Povinelli, 2003; Breckenridge, 1995; Appadurai, 1996.
2  Warner (2002: 11) writes that we recognize people we don't know as members of our world because we are related to them as "transient participants in common publics." Through the circulation of text and digital maneuvers, smaller communities of affect emerge. Here, I make a scalar and affective distinction between publics and community.
3  More recently, there is a shift toward microblogging, as noted by Lenhart and Fox, 2006.
4  On racial politics in the food-blog space see Mannur, 2013.
5  Foodworld, a food-blog aggregator, maintained by one of the bloggers, lists

blogs on Indian food written mainly by South Asian bloggers. http://food world.redchillies.us.

6 Sandeepa. Bong Mom's CookBook Recipe Index. Bong Mom's Cookbook. http://www.bongcookbook.com/2008/12/recipe-index.html.

7 Jay, K. Sumadhura. http://kiranjay.blogspot.com/p/about.me.html.

8 Indira. Mahanandi. http://www.nandyala.org/mahanandi/about.

9 Indosungod. Daily Musings. http://indosungod.blogspot.com/p/about.html.

10 Manisha. But I Am Home. Indian Food Rocks. http://www.indianfoodrocks. com/2011/02/but-i-am-home.html.

11 Namitha. Collaborative Curry. http://www.collaborativecurry.com/2009/09/ spinach-paalak-thoran.html.

12 Manisha. The Last Bastion. Indian Food Rocks. http://www.indianfoodrocks. com/2008/03/last-bastion.html.

13 Reader comment (Rita Mosquita). Indian Food Rocks. http://www.indian foodrocks.com/2008/03/last-bastion.html.

14 Meena. Hooked on Heat. http://www.hookedonheat.com/indian-cooking-101.

15 Manisha. And That's Indian, You Say? Indian Food Rocks. http://www.indian foodrocks.com/2012/01/and-thats-indian-you-say.html.

16 Nivedita. Interview via Skype, February 21, 2012.

17 Nivedita. Carrot Halwa Blondie Bars – an Update. Panfusine. http://www. panfusine.com/2012/01/carrot-halwa-blondie-bars-update.html.

18 Nivedita. Interview via Skype, February 21, 2012.

19 Vaishali. Holy Cow. http://www.holycowvegan.net/p/about-me.html.

20 Basu, M. Interview via Skype, February 9, 2012.

21 Basu, M. Interview via Skype, February 9, 2012.

22 Interview with Mallika Basu: Just Books, 2010.

23 Sandeepa. Slowing Down the Network. Bong Mom's Cookbook. http://www. bongcookbook.com/2011/01/slowing-down-network.html.

24 Manisha. Interview via Skype, February 15, 2012.

25 In February 2015, the Obama administration finalized rules that would selectively allow spouses of high-skilled foreign workers to work in the United States. See O'Brien, 2015.

26 Manisha. Food Blogger's Meme. Indian Food Rocks. http://www.indian foodrocks.com/2006/04/food-bloggers-meme.html.

27 In the Indian context, where dining across caste boundaries might be a delicate matter, Appadurai (1988: 7) writes that recipes move where people may not. Here, we see a global variation. See also Mannur (2005) for an insightful analysis.

28 On the disconnect between exoticized perceptions of cultural products and the life of immigrants, see Rubin and Melnick, 2007.

### Chapter 6 Authenticity: Pursuits of Auras

1 All three areas named here – Astoria (New York City Borough of Queens), Kreuzberg (western part of Berlin), and Southall (London Borough of Ealing)

– have highly diverse immigrant populations. While each has a distinct history, they all serve as examples of how immigrants create networked cultures and activities in global cities like New York, London, and Berlin. For some examples of ethnographies related to these spaces, see Margolis, 1993; Mandel, 2008; Hall, 2002.

2 Mulholland, 2014b.

3 See report of Marine Le Pen's interview with the Europe 1 radio station in Mulholland, 2014a.

4 America's Favorite National Pastime: Hating Soccer. http://www.anncoulter.com/columns/2014-06-25.html.

5 For the interview with Tebbit, see Fisher, 1990.

6 Nir, Cohen, and Rashbaum, 2013.

7 ABC News, 2014.

8 Bloomberg News, 2013.

9 BlouinArtInfo, 2013.

10 For a philosophically grounded discussion of the ideal form as intrinsic to the notion of authenticity, see Lowney (2009).

11 The history of authenticity, its links to structures of modernity, and its evolution from the notion of sincerity and being true to one's self are explored at length by Trilling (1972). I focus here much more on the place of authenticity in its current iteration in terms of value, media, and the global flow of commodities, drawing on reproduction in Walter Benjamin's terms.

12 This surge of interest in Carnatic music in North America marks a digital moment in the history of a much longer discourse associated with this classical style with regard to its pedagogy, reproducibility, and contested relationship with colonialism. So here is a style that on the surface seems apparently esoteric and closed, but has already had its global encounters with the colonial gaze of the West (see Weidman, 2006). The new global circulation of this music comes with the mobility of the south Indian diaspora.

13 See also Khandelwal, 1995.

14 For popular reportage see Melwani, 2014.

15 There is a vibrant South Asian hip-hop culture, for example, that has been well documented. See Sharma, 2010; Purkayastha, 2005.

16 Discussing the circulation of Hindu nationalism in the diaspora, Rajagopal (2001) notes that expatriate nationalism has a social basis different from that of its adherents in the homeland. In the case discussed here, music becomes a performance of cultural expatriate citizenship,

17 Ganapathy, 2010.

18 Subramanian, S., 2008.

19 Interview with Vidya Subramanian. http://mycarnatic.org/podcastplayer/?title=15.

20 Ravindran, 2010.

21 Suhasini, 2010.

22 *Gurukul* is the short form of *gurukulavasa*, the Sanskrit term that captures the

pedagogical method whereby the student learnt through living in the guru or teacher's home and studying the art through imitation.

23 Shashikiran, 2010.
24 Weidman, 2006.
25 Subramaniam, S., 2006.
26 Ravindran, 2010.
27 Santhanagopalan, 2010.
28 Ramakrishnan, 2010.
29 Interview with V. V. Sundaram. http://www.aradhana.org/sampradaya/2009.
30 Ravindran, 2010.
31 The term "NRI" (non-resident Indian) is a category created by the Indian government and is now widely used. This was mentioned in the introduction and is taken up later, in the concluding chapter.
32 Narayan, 2010. Chennai is regarded as one of the important centers of Carnatic music in south India; other centers include Bangalore, Hyderabad, and Thiruvananthapuram.

**Chapter 7  Conclusion: Destinations and Beginnings**
1 Luibhéid (2002) discusses how sexual policing in US immigration policy has historically viewed certain types of sexuality as being threatening to national security.
2 Crouch, 2005.
3 On this point see Hegde, 2011; Grewal and Kaplan, 2001.
4 Brown, 2010.
5 On this subject, there has been a considerable amount of scholarship, as noted in chapter 3. Also on this subject, see Maira, 2009; Kundnani, 2014.
6 *Time*, 1985.
7 Henry, Mehta, Monroe, and Winbush, 1990, quoted in Chavez, L., 2001: 138.
8 Sun, 2012.
9 http://blog.tides.org/2012/06/19/tides-project-define-american-on-cover-of-time-magazine.
10 Behdad, 2005; Ngai, 2003.
11 On this point see Löbbermann's (2003) essay on the narrative techniques of tourism in New York and the semiotic strategies through which the touristic space is produced.
12 Cuming-Bruce and Erlanger, 2009.
13 Goodstein, 2010; Gowen, 2010.
14 For details of this see Finnegan, 2006.
15 Bryant, 2014.
16 Anderson (1998) noted that as a result of mass migrations and communication, members of a national group can maintain political connections with nationalist movements in the home country. While Anderson focuses on the diaspora as independent actors, Mani and Varadarajan (2005) argue that more recently

states actively constitute diasporas as national subjects, thereby redefining the domain of the national. In the New York City event described, Modi once again tweaked and reworked this connection.

17 Gonzalez-Barrera and Krogstad, 2014.
18 On this issue, see Golash-Boza, 2014. Also, listen to a radio documentary on this subject: This American Life from WBEZ, 2014.
19 On this subject of selling designer *hijab*s online and using the diasporic turn to wearing Muslim head cover as an entrepreneurial space, see Tarlo, 2010.
20 Penketh and Borger, 2015.
21 Schuessler, 2015.
22 Keane, 2015.
23 Yuhas, 2015.
24 On methodological nationalism, see Wimmer and Glick Schiller, 2002.

# References

ABC News (July 15, 2014) Video: Alleged Master Art Forger Found in Shanghai. *ABC News.* http://abcnews.go.com/WNT/video/alleged-master-art-forger-found-shanghai-24575788.

Abu-Lughod, L. (2002) Do Muslim Women Really Need Saving? Anthropological Reflections on Cultural Relativism and its Others. *American Anthropologist* 104(3), 783–90.

Abu-Lughod, L. (2013) *Do Muslim Women Need Saving?* Harvard University Press, Cambridge, MA.

Adichie, C. N. (2013) *Americanah.* Knopf, New York, NY. (Kindle edition)

Agamben, G. (1998) *Homo Sacer: Sovereign Power and Bare Life.* Heller-Roazen, D. (trans.). University of Minnesota Press, Minneapolis, MN.

Ahmed, L. (1993) *Women and Gender in Islam: Historical Roots of a Modern Debate.* Yale University Press, New Haven, CT.

Ahmed, S. (2004) *The Cultural Politics of Emotion.* Routledge, New York, NY, and London, UK.

Alonso, A. and Oiarzabal, P. J. (eds.) (2010) *Diasporas in the New Media Age: Identity, Politics and Community.* University of Nevada Press, Las Vegas, NV.

Amin, A. (2012) *Land of Strangers.* Polity, Cambridge, UK.

Anderson, B. (1991) *Imagined Communities: Reflections on the Origin and Spread of Nationalism.* Verso, New York, NY.

Anderson, B. (1998) *The Spectre of Comparisons: Nationalisms, Southeast Asia, and the World.* Verso, New York, NY.

Anonymous (April 19, 2013) Police on Scanner Identify the Names of #Boston Marathon Suspects in Gunfight, Suspect 1: Mike Mulugeta. Suspect 2: Sunil Tripathi. *Twitter.* https://twitter.com/YourAnonNews/status/32514184 0561074176.

Appadurai, A. (1988) How to Make a National Cuisine: Cookbooks in Contemporary India. *Comparative Studies in Society and History* 30(1), 3–24.

Appadurai, A. (1996) *Modernity at Large: Cultural Dimensions of Globalization.* University of Minnesota Press, Minneapolis, MN.

Appadurai, A. (2006) *Fear of Small Numbers: An Essay on the Geography of Anger.* Duke University Press, Durham, NC.

Appadurai, A. (2010) How Histories Make Geographies. *Transcultural Studies* 1. http://journals.ub.uni-heidelberg.de/index.php/transcultural/article/view/6129.

Apuzzo, M. and Goldman, A. (October 26, 2011) NYPD Keeps Files on Muslims

Who Change Their Names. *AP*. http://www.ap.org/Content/AP-In-The-News/2011/NYPD-keeps-files-on-Muslims-who-change-their-names.

Armstrong, K. (October 26, 2006) My Years in a Habit Taught Me the Paradox of Veiling. *Guardian*. http://www.theguardian.com/commentisfree/2006/oct/26/comment.politics1.

Asen, R. and Brouwer, D. C. (eds.) (2001) *Counterpublics and the State*. State University of New York Press, Albany, NY.

Astor, A. (2009) Unauthorized Immigration, Securitization and the Making of Operation Wetback. *Latino Studies* 7(1), 5–29.

Axel, B. K. (2002) The Diasporic Imaginary. *Public Culture* 14(2), 411–28.

Ayotte, K. J. and Husain, M. E. (2005) Securing Afghan Women: Neocolonialism, Epistemic Violence, and the Rhetoric of the Veil. *NWSA Journal* 17(3), 112–33.

Azoulay, A. (2008) *The Civil Contract of Photography*. Zone Books, New York, NY.

Azoulay, A. (2012) *Civil Imagination: A Political Ontology of Photography*. Verso, New York, NY.

Bada, X., Fox, J., and Selee, A. (2006) Preface. In: Bada, X., Fox, J., and Selee, A. (eds.) *Invisible No More: Mexican Migrant Civic Participation in the United States*, pp. v–vi. http://www.wilsoncenter.org/publication/invisible-no-more-mexican-migrant-civic-participation-the-united-states.

Bailey, O., Georgiou, M., and Harindranath, R. (eds.) (2007) *Transnational Lives and Media: Re-Imagining Diasporas*. Palgrave Macmillan, New York, NY.

Baker, B. and Rytina, N. (March 2013) Estimates of the Unauthorized Immigrant Population Residing in the United States: January 2012. *Population Estimates*. http://www.dhs.gov/sites/default/files/publications/ois_ill_pe_2012_2.pdf.

Balibar, E. (1991) Es Gibt Keinen Staat in Europa: Racism and Politics in Europe Today. *New Left Review* 186, 5–19.

Balibar, E. (2000) What We Owe to the Sans-Papiers. In: Guenther, L. and Heesters, C. (eds.) *Social Insecurity*. Anasi, Toronto, Canada, pp. 42–3.

Banerji, C. (2007) *Eating India: An Odyssey into the Food and Culture of the Land of Spices*. Bloomsbury, New York, NY.

Bar-tur, Y. (April 22, 2013) Boston Police Schooled Us All on Social Media. *Mashable*. http://mashable.com/2013/04/22/boston-police-social-media.

Basu, M. (2010) *Miss Masala: Real Indian Cooking for Busy Living*. HarperCollins, London, UK.

Baudrillard, J. (1998) *The Consumer Society: Myths and Structures*. Sage, London, UK.

Bauman, Z. (2003) *Wasted Lives: Modernity and Its Outcastes*. Polity, Cambridge, UK.

Bauman, Z. (2006) *Liquid Times: Living in an Age of Uncertainty*. Polity, Cambridge, UK.

BBC News (October 6, 2006a) "Remove Full Veils" Urges Straw. *BBC*. http://news.bbc.co.uk/2/hi/uk_news/politics/5411954.stm.

BBC News (October 15, 2006b) Davis in "UK Apartheid" Warning. *BBC*. http://news.bbc.co.uk/1/hi/uk/6052232.stm.

BBC News (November 2, 2006c) Muslims Must Feel British – Straw. *BBC*. http://news.bbc.co.uk/2/hi/uk_news/politics/6110798.stm.

Beamon, T. and Bachman, J. (July 18, 2013) Rep. Steve King Slams Norquist over Attacks on Immigration. *Newsmax*. http://www.newsmax.com/Newsfront/king-norquistattackimmigration/2013/07/18/id/515882.

Behdad, A. (2005) *A Forgetful Nation: On Immigration and Cultural Identity in the United States*. Duke University Press, Durham, NC.

Belluck, P. (July 1, 2000) Mexican Presidential Candidates Campaign in U.S. *New York Times*. http://www.nytimes.com/2000/07/01/world/mexican-presidential-candidates-campaign-in-us.html.

Benhabib, S. (2002) *The Claims of Culture: Equality and Diversity in the Global Era*. Princeton University Press, Princeton, NJ.

Benítez, J. L. (2006) Transnational Dimensions of the Digital Divide among Salvadoran Immigrants in the Washington DC Metropolitan Area. *Global Networks* 6(2), 181–99.

Benjamin, W. (1968) The Work of Art in the Age of Mechanical Reproduction. In: Arendt, H. (ed.), Zohn, H. (trans.) *Illuminations: Essays and Reflections*. Shocken Books, New York, NY, pp. 217–51.

Benson, R. (2013) *Shaping Immigration News: A French-American Comparison*. Cambridge University Press, New York, NY.

Berlant, L. (1997) *The Queen of America Goes to Washington: Essays on Sex and Citizenship*. Duke University Press, Durham, NC.

Berlant, L. and Warner, M. (1998) Sex in Public. *Critical Inquiry* 24(2), 547–66.

Bernal, V. (2006) Eritrea On-Line: Diaspora, Cyberspace and the Public Sphere. *American Ethnologist* 32(4), 660–75.

Blair, T. (December 8, 2006) The Duty to Integrate: Shared British Values. http://webarchive.nationalarchives.gov.uk/20130109092234/http://www.number10.gov.uk/Page10563.

Bloomberg News (December 19, 2013) The Other Side of an $80 Million Art Fraud: A Master Forger Speaks. *Bloomberg Business*. http://www.businessweek.com/articles/2013-12-19/the-other-side-of-an-800-million-art-fraud-a-master-forger-speaks#p2.

Blouin ArtInfo (August 19, 2013) Master Forger Behind Knoedler Fakes Identified as Chinese Artist Pei-Shen Qian. *Blouin ArtInfo*. http://blogs.artinfo.com/artintheair/2013/08/19/master-forger-behind-knoedler-fakes-identified-as-chinese-artist-pei-shen-qian.

Bogado, A. (July 2, 2013) Coming Out of the Shadows in Union Square. *Nation*. http://www.thenation.com/blog/173587/coming-out-shadows-union-square#.

boyd, d. (2006) A Blogger's Blog: Exploring the Definition of a Medium. *Reconstruction* 6(4). http://www.danah.org/papers/ABloggersBlog.pdf.

boyd, d. (2011) Social Network Sites as Networked Publics: Affordances, Dynamics and Implications. In: Papacharissi, Z. A. (ed.) *Networked Self: Identity, Community and Culture on Social Network Sites*. Routledge, New York, NY, pp. 39–58.

Brah, A. (1996) *Cartographies of Diaspora: Contesting Identities*. Routledge, London, UK.

Breckenridge, C. A. (1995) *Consuming Modernity: Public Culture in Contemporary India*. University of Minnesota Press, Minneapolis, MN.

Brettell, C. B. and Hollifield, J. F. (eds.) (2000) *Migration Theory: Talking Across Disciplines*. Routledge, New York, NY.

Brinkerhoff, J. M. (2009) *Digital Diasporas: Identity and Transnational Engagement*. Cambridge University Press, Cambridge, UK, and New York, NY.

Brouwer, D. C. and Asen, R. (2010) Public Modalities or the Metaphors We Theorize. In: Brouwer, D. C. and Asen, R. (eds.) *Public Modalities*. University of Alabama Press, Tuscaloosa, AL, pp. 1–33.

Brown, W. (2005) *Edgework: Critical Essays in Knowledge and Politics*. Princeton University Press, Princeton, NJ.

Brown, W. (2010) *Walled States, Waning Sovereignty*. Zone Books, New York, NY.

Bryant, N. (September 28, 2014) New York Gives Star Treatment to Indian PM, Modi. *BBC*. http://www.bbc.com/news/world-us-canada-29405462.

Buettner, E. (2008) "Going for an Indian": South Asian Restaurants and the Limits of Multiculturalism in Britain. *Journal of Modern History* 80(4), 865–901.

Bunting, M. (October 8, 2006) Jack Straw Has Unleashed a Storm of Prejudice and Intensified Division. *Guardian*. http://www.theguardian.com/commentisfree/2006/oct/09/comment.politics.

Butler, J. (1993) *Bodies that Matter: On the Discursive Limits of Sex*. Routledge, New York, NY.

Butler, J. and Athanasiou, A. (2013) *Dispossession: The Performative in the Political*. Polity, Cambridge, UK. (Kindle edition)

Cacho, L. M. (2012) *Social Death: Racialized Rightlessness and the Criminalization of the Unprotected*. NYU Press, New York.

Caminero-Santangelo, M. (2012) Documenting the Undocumented: Life Narratives of Unauthorized Immigrants. *Biography* 35(3), 449–71.

Castles, S. (2002) Migration and Community Formation Under Conditions of Globalization. *International Migration Review* 36(4), 1143–68.

Castles, S., de Haas, H., and Miller, M. J. (2013) *The Age of Migration: International Population Movements in the Modern World*. Palgrave Macmillan, New York, NY.

Chakrabarty, D. (2000) *Provincializing Europe: Postcolonial Thought and Historical Difference*. Princeton University Press, Princeton, NJ.

Challapalli, S. (August 4, 2006) Hot Off the . . . Blog! *Hindu Business Line*. http://www.thehindubusinessline.in/life/2006/08/04/stories/2006080400020100.htm.

Chavez, K. R. (2013) *Queer Migration Politics: Activist Rhetoric and Coalitional Possibilities*. University of Illinois Press, Urbana-Champaign, IL.

Chavez, L. (2001) *Covering Immigration: Popular Images and the Politics of the Nation*. University of California Press, Berkeley, CA.

Chavez, L. (2013) *The Latino Threat: Constructing Immigrants, Citizens and the Nation*. Stanford University Press, Stanford, CA.

Chen, A. (April 17, 2013) Your Guide to the Boston Marathon Bombing Amateur Internet Crowd-Sleuthing. *Gawker*. http://gawker.com/5994892/your-guide-to-the-boston-marathon-bombing-amateur-internet-crowd-sleuthing.

Chow, R. (2006) *The Age of the World Target: Self-Referentiality in War, Theory, and Comparative Work*. Duke University Press, Durham, NC.

Clifford, J. (1997) *Routes: Travel and Translation in the Late Twentieth Century*. Harvard University Press, Cambridge, MA.

Coleman, E. G. (2010) Ethnographic Approaches to Digital Media. *Annual Review of Anthropology* 39(1), 487–505.

Couldry, N. (2008) Mediatization or Mediation? Alternative Understandings of the Emergent Space of Digital Storytelling. *New Media and Society* 10(3), 373–91.

Couldry, N. and McCarthy, A. (2004) Introduction. In: Couldry, N. and McCarthy, A. (eds.) *Mediaspace: Place, Scale and Culture in a Media Age*. Routledge, New York, NY, pp. 1–18.

Coutin, S. B. (2005) Being En Route. *American Anthropologist* 107(2), 195–206.

Coutin, S. B. (2011) The Rights of Non-Citizens in the United States. *Annual Review of Law and Social Science* 7(1), 289–308.

Coutin, S. B. (2013) Cultural Logics of Belonging and Nationalism: Transnationalism, Naturalization, and U.S. Immigration Policies. *American Ethnologist* 30(4), 508–28.

Cowell, A. (October 18, 2006a) Blair Criticizes Full Islamic Veils as "Mark of Separation." *New York Times*. http://www.nytimes.com/2006/10/18/world/europe/18britain.html.

Cowell, A. (October 22, 2006b) For Multiculturalist Britain, Uncomfortable New Clothes. *New York Times*. http://www.nytimes.com/2006/10/22/world/europe/22iht-web.1022britain.3243679.html.

Crouch, G. (November 16, 2005) Dutch Immigration Kit Offers a Revealing View. *New York Times*. http://www.nytimes.com/2006/03/16/world/europe/16iht-dutch5852942.html?_r=1&.

Crouch, I. (July 17, 2013) The Inconvenient Image of Dzhohkar Tsarnaev. *New Yorker*. http://www.newyorker.com/online/blogs/newsdesk/2013/07/dzhokhar-tsarnaev-rolling-stone-cover-controversy.html.

Cuming-Bruce, N. and Erlanger, E. (November 29, 2009) Swiss Ban Building of Minarets on Mosques. *New York Times*. http://www.nytimes.com/2009/11/30/world/europe/30swiss.html.

Cunningham, S. and Sinclair, J. (eds.) (2001) *Floating Lives: The Media and Asian Diasporas*. Rowman & Littlefield, Oxford, UK.

Cyndi (2012) Personal Story. In: Manuel, J., Pineda, C., Galisky, A., and Shine, R. (eds.) *Papers: Stories by Undocumented Youth*. Graham Street Productions, Portland, OR, p. 12.

Datta, S. M. (2013) *Bong Mom's Cookbook*. HarperCollins, Noida, India.

De Certeau, M. (1984) *The Practice of Everyday Life*. Rendall, S. F. (trans.). University of California Press, Berkeley, CA.

De Genova, N. (2005) *Working the Boundaries: Race, Space and "Illegality" in Mexican Chicago*. Duke University Press, Durham, NC.

De Genova, N. (2009) Conflicts of Mobility, and the Mobility of Conflict: Rightlessness, Presence, Subjectivity, Freedom. *Subjectivity* 29(1), 445–66.

De Genova, N. (2010) The Queer Politics of Migration: Reflections on "Illegality" and Incorrigibility. *Studies in Social Justice* 4(2), 101–26.

De Haas, H. (2008) The Myth of Invasion: The Inconvenient Realities of African Migration to Europe. *Third World Quarterly* 29(7), 1305–22.

Dean, J. (2010) *Blog Theory: Feedback and Capture in the Circuits of Drive*. Polity, Cambridge, UK.

Dembour, M. and Kelly, T. (2011) *Are Human Rights for Migrants? Critical Reflections on the Status of Irregular Migrants in Europe and the United States*. Routledge, New York, NY.

Deuze, M. (2012) *Media Life*. Polity, Cambridge, UK.

Diminescu, D. (2008) The Connected Migrant: An Epistemological Manifesto. *Social Science Information* 47(4), 565–79.

Diminescu, D. and Loveluck, B. (2014) Traces of Dispersion: Online Media and Diasporic Identities. *Crossings: Journal of Migration and Culture* 5(1), 23–39.

Douglas, M. (1978) *Purity and Danger: An Analysis of the Concepts of Pollution and Taboo*. Routledge, New York, NY.

Durbin, D. (June 28, 2011) Passing the DREAM Act. http://www.durbin.senate.gov/public/index.cfm/hot-topics?ContentRecord_id=43eaa136-a3de-4d72-bc1b-12c3000f0ae9.

Dyer, R. (2002) Immigration, Postwar London, and the Politics of Everyday Life in Sam Selvon's Fiction. *Cultural Critique* 52, 108–44.

Echchaibi, N. (1999) (Be)Longing Media: Minority Radio Between Cultural Retention and Renewal. The Case of Beur FM and Radio Multikulti. *Javnost/ The Public* 9(1), 37–50.

Echchaibi, N. (2011) *Voicing Diasporas: Ethnic Radio in Paris and Berlin between Cultural Renewal and Retention*. Lexington Books, Lanham, MD.

Elliott, B. S., Gerber, D. A., and Sinke, S. M. (2006) *Letters across Borders: The Epistolary Practices of International Migrants*. Palgrave Macmillan, New York, NY.

El-Tayeb, F. (2011) *European Others: Queering Ethnicity in Postnational Europe*. University of Minnesota Press, Minneapolis, MN.

Ezekiel, J. (2006) French Dressing: Race, Gender, and the Hijab Story. *Feminist Studies* 32(2), 256–78.

Fazal, S. and Tsagarousianou, R. (2002) Diasporic Communication: Transnational Cultural Practices and Communicative Spaces. *Javnost/ The Public* 9(1), 5–18.

Feldman, A. (1994) On Cultural Aesthesia: From Desert Storm to Rodney King. *American Ethnologist* 21(2), 404–18.

Feldman, A. (2005) The Actuarial Gaze: From 9/11 to Abu Ghraib. *Cultural Studies* 19(2), 203– 26.

Finnegan, W. (December 5, 2006) New in Town. *New Yorker*, p. 46. http://www.newyorker.com/magazine/2006/12/11/new-in-town-2.

Fisher, D. (April 19, 1990) Split Between Britain, U.S. Seen as "Inevitable": Foreign Policy: The Conservative Party Chairman Fears that a "Less European" America Will Provide the Wedge. *Los Angeles Times.* http://articles.latimes.com/1990-04-19/news/mn-2009_1_conservative-party.

Flanders, L. (April 6, 2013) Coming Out of the Shadows: Undocumented, Unafraid and Unapologetic. *GRITtv.* http://grittv.org/?video=out-of-the-shadows-emerges-a-new-generation-of-immigrant-youth.

Fortunati, L., Pertierra, R., and Vincent, J. (2013) Introduction: Migrations and Diasporas: Making Their World Elsewhere. In: Fortunati, L. and Pertierra, R. (eds.) *Migration, Diaspora and Information Technology in Global Societies.* Routledge, New York, pp. 1–20.

Foucault, M. (1977) *Discipline and Punish: The Birth of the Prison.* Pantheon Books, New York, NY.

Fraser, N. (March 2005) Transnationalizing the Public Sphere. http://www.republicart.net/disc/publicum/fraser01_en.htm.

Freedman, S. (August 10, 2012) If the Sikh Temple Had Been a Mosque. *New York Times.* http://www.nytimes.com/2012/08/11/us/if-the-sikh-temple-had-been-a-muslim-mosque-on-religion.html?pagewanted=all&_r=0.

Fuchs, E. (June 27, 2013) INDICTMENT: Boston Bombing Suspect Ran Over His Brother While a Cop Was Trying to Drag Him to Safety. *Business Insider.* http://www.businessinsider.com/how-tamerlan-tsarnaev-died-2013-6.

Fung, K. and Mirkinson, J. (April 18, 2013) New York Post's Boston "Bag Men" Front Page Called "A New Low," "Appalling." *Huff Post.* http://www.huffingtonpost.com/2013/04/18/ny-post-boston-suspects-bag-men-front-page_n_3109052.html.

Gajjala, R. (2010) 3D Indian (Digital) Diasporas. In: Alonso, A. and Oiarzabal, P. (eds.) *Diasporas in the New Media Age.* University of Nevada Press, Las Vegas, NV, pp. 209–24.

Gajjala, R. and Gajjala, V. (2008) *South Asian Technospaces.* Peter Lang, New York, NY.

Galisky, A. (2009) Papers. http://www.papersthemovie.com. (Documentary project)

Gammeltoft-Hansen, T. (April 1, 2012) Can Privatization Kill? *New York Times.* http://www.nytimes.com/2012/04/02/opinion/when-it-comes-to-immigration-privatization-can-kill.html?_r=0&module=ArrowsNav&contentCollection=Opinion&action=keypress&region=FixedLeft&pgtype=articleem.

Ganapathy, L. (April 12, 2010) The Cleveland Aradhana, a Marvel. *Hindu.* http://www.thehindu.com/arts/article394764.ece.

Gaonkar, D. P. and Povinelli, E. A. (2003) Technologies of Public Forms: Circulation, Transfiguration, Recognition. *Public Culture* 15(3), 385–97.

Gardner, A. (2012) Why Do They Keep Coming? Labor Migrants in the Persian Gulf States. In: Kamreva, M. and Babar, Z. (eds.) *Migrant Labor in the Persian Gulf*. Columbia University Press, New York, NY, pp. 41–58.

Gates, K. A. (2011) *Our Biometric Future: Facial Recognition Technology and the Culture of Surveillance*. NYU Press, New York, NY.

Georgiou, M. (2006) *Diaspora, Identity and the Media: Diasporic Transnationalism and Mediated Spatialities*. Hampton Press, Cresskill, NJ.

Georgiou, M. (2014) *Media and the City*. Polity, Cambridge, UK.

Gerbaudo, P. (2012) *Tweets and the Street: Social Media and Contemporary Activism*. Pluto Press, New York, NY.

Gillespie, M. (1995) *Television, Ethnicity and Cultural Change*. Routledge, London, UK.

Gilroy, P. (2004) *Postcolonial Melancholia*. Columbia University Press, New York, NY.

Gitelman, L. (2014) *Paper Knowledge: Toward a Media History of Documents*. Duke University Press, Durham, NC.

Glick-Schiller, N., Basch, L., and Szanton-Blanc, C. (1995) From Immigrant to Transmigrant: Theorizing Transnational Migration. *Anthropological Quarterly* 68(1), 48–63.

Golash-Boza, T. (2014) Tattoos, Stigma, and National Identity among Guatemalan Deportees. In: Gleeson, S. and Park, J. S. W. (eds.) *The Nation and its Peoples: Citizens, Denizens, Migrants*. Routledge, New York, NY, pp. 203–22.

Göle, N. (2006) Islam Resetting the European Agenda? *Public Culture* 18(1), 11–14.

Gonzalez-Barrera, A. and Krogstad, J. M. (October 2, 2014) U.S. Deportations of Immigrants Reach Record High in 2013. *Pew Research Center*. http://www.pewresearch.org/fact-tank/2014/10/02/u-s-deportations-of-immigrants-reach-record-high-in-2013.

Goodstein, L. (August 7, 2010) Across Nation, Mosque Projects Meet Opposition. *New York Times*. http://www.nytimes.com/2010/08/08/us/08mosque.html

Gopinath, G. (2005) *Impossible Desires: Queer Diasporas and South Asian Public Cultures*. Duke University Press, Durham, NC.

Gowen, A. (August 23, 2010) Far from Ground Zero, Other Plans for Mosques Run into Vehement Opposition. *Washington Post*. http://www.washingtonpost.com/wp-dyn/content/article/2010/08/22/AR2010082202895.html.

Greenfield, R. (July 25, 2013) Reddit Karma Doesn't Work in Real Life: Lessons of the Sunil Triapthi Debacle. *Wire*. http://www.thewire.com/technology/2013/07/reddit-karma-sunil-triapthi-debacle/67594.

Grewal, I. and Kaplan, C. (2001) Global Identities: Theorizing Transnational Studies of Sexuality. *GLQ: A Journal of Lesbian and Gay Studies* 7(4), 663–79.

Grossberg, L. (1992) *We Gotta Get Out of This Place: Popular Conservatism and Postmodern Culture*. Routledge, New York, NY.

Grossberg, L. (1993) Can Cultural Studies Find True Happiness in Communication? *Journal of Communication* 43(4), 89–97.

Guilbault, J. (2005) Audible Entanglement: Nation and Diasporas in Trinidad's Calypso Music Scene. *Small Axe* 17(1), 40–63.

Guterl, M. P. (2013) *Seeing Race in Modern America*. University of North Carolina Press, Chapel Hill, NC.

Haldrup, M., Koefoed, L., and Simonsen, K. (2008) Practicing Fear: Encountering O/other Bodies. In: Pain, R. and Smith, S. (eds.) *Fear: Critical Geopolitics and Everyday Life*. Routledge, New York, NY, pp. 117–28.

Hall, K. (2002) *Lives in Translation: Sikh Youth as British Citizens*. University of Pennsylvania Press, Philadelphia, PA.

Hamid, M. (2007) *The Reluctant Fundamentalist*. Harcourt, New York, NY.

Hansen, K. (1996) Performing Identities: Tyagaraja Music Festivals in North America. *South Asia Research* 16(2), 155–74.

Hansen, M. (2008) Benjamin's Aura. *Critical Inquiry* 34(2), 336–75.

Harring, S. L. (2000) The Diallo Verdict: Another "Tragic Accident" in New York's War on Street Crime? *Social Justice* 27(1), 9–18.

Hegde, R. S. (1998) Swinging the Trapeze: The Negotiation of Identity among Asian Indian Women in the United States. In: Gonzalez, A. and Tanno, D. (eds.) *Communication and Identity across Cultures*. Sage, Thousand Oaks, CA, pp. 34–56.

Hegde, R. S. (2011) Introduction. In: Hegde, R. S. (ed.) *Circuits of Visibility: Gender and Transnational Media Cultures*. NYU Press, New York, NY, pp. 1–17.

Henry, W., III, Mehta, N., Monroe, S., and Winbush, D. (April 9, 1990) Beyond the Melting Pot. *Time*.

Honig, B. (2001) *Democracy and the Foreigner*. Princeton University Press, Princeton, NJ.

Horst, H. (2006) The Blessings and Burdens of Communication: The Cell Phone in Jamaican Transnational Social Fields. *Global Networks: A Journal of Transnational Affairs* 6(2), 143–59.

Horsti, K. (2003) Global Mobility and the Media: Presenting Asylum Seekers as a Threat. *Nordicom Review* 24(1), 41–54.

Horsti, K. (2008) Europeanisation of Public Debate: Swedish and Finnish News on African Migration to Spain. *Javnost/ The Public* 4, 41–54.

Horsti, K. (2013) De-Ethnicized Victims: Mediatized Advocacy for Asylum Seekers. *Journalism: Theory, Practice & Criticism* 14(1), 78–95.

*Huff Post* (July 17, 2013) John King: Boston Bombing Suspect A "Dark-Skinned Male." *Huff Post*. http://www.huffingtonpost.com/2013/04/17/john-king-boston-bombing-dark-skinned-male-ifill_n_3102195.html.

Inda, J. X. (2005) *Targeting Immigrants: Government, Technology, and Ethics*. Blackwell, Malden, MA.

Isin, E. F. (2002) *Being Political: Genealogies of Citizenship*. University of Minnesota Press, Minneapolis, MN.

Isin, E. F. (2004) The Neurotic Citizen. *Citizenship Studies* 8(3), 217–35.

Isin, E. F. (2008) Theorizing Acts of Citizenship. In: Isin, E. F. and Nielsen, G. M. (eds.) *Acts of Citizenship*. Zed Books, New York, NY, pp. 15–43.

Jaffrey, M. (1975) *An Invitation to Indian Cooking*. Knopf, New York, NY.

Jameson, F. (1999) Notes on Globalization as a Philosophical Issue. In: Jameson, F. and Miyoshi, M. (eds.) *The Cultures of Globalization*. Duke University Press, Durham, NC, pp. 54–80.

Jayal, N. G. (2013) *Citizenship and Its Discontents: An Indian History*. Harvard University Press, Cambridge, MA. (Kindle edition)

Johnston, P. (December 9, 2006) Adopt Our Values or Stay Away, Says Blair. *Telegraph*. http://www.telegraph.co.uk/news/uknews/1536408/Adopt-our-values-or-stay-away-says-Blair.html.

Just Books (July 31, 2010) Malika Basu on 'Miss Masala'. *NDTV*. http://www.ndtv.com/video/player/just-books/mallika-basu-on-miss-masala/155692.

Kang, J. C. (July 25, 2013) Should Reddit Be Blamed for the Spreading of a Smear? *New York Times*. http://www.nytimes.com/2013/07/28/magazine/should-reddit-be-blamed-for-the-spreading-of-a-smear.html?_r=0.

Kapur, R. (2005) Travel Plans: Border Crossings and the Rights of Transnational Migrants. *Harvard Human Rights Journal* 18, 107–38.

Karim, K. (2002) *The Media of Diaspora*. Routledge, London, UK.

Keane, E. (April 29, 2015). Charlie Hebdo and the PEN Award: Petition Sent to Authors Urging Them to "Disassociate Ourselves" from Honoring the Magazine. *Salon*. http://www.salon.com/2015/04/29/charlie_hebdo_and_the_pen_award_petition_sent_to_authors_urging_them_to_disassociate_ourselves_from_honoring_the_magazine.

Keller, J. (April 26, 2013) How Boston Police Won the Twitter Wars During the Marathon Bomber Hunt. *Business Week*. http://www.businessweek.com/articles/2013-04-26/how-boston-police-won-the-twitter-wars-during-bomber-hunt

Khandelwal, M. S. (1995) Indian Immigrants in Queens, New York City: Patterns of Spatial Concentration and Distribution, 1965–1990. In: Van der Veer, P. (ed.) *Nation and Migration: The Politics of Space in the South Asian Diaspora*. University of Pennsylvania Press, Philadelphia, PA, pp. 178–96.

Kilgannon, C. and Schmidt, M. S. (May 2, 2010) Vendors Who Alerted Police Called Heroes. *New York Times*. http://www.nytimes.com/2010/05/03/nyregion/03vendor.html.

King, R. and Wood, N. (2001) *Media and Migration: Constructions of Mobility and Difference*. Routledge, London, UK.

Koopmans, R., Statham, P., Giugni, M., and Passy, F. (2005) *Contested Citizenship: Immigration and Cultural Diversity in Europe*. University of Minnesota Press, Minneapolis, MN.

Koshy, S. (2008) Introduction. In: Koshy, S. and Radhakrishnan, S. (eds.) *Transnational South Asians: The Making of a Neo-Diaspora*. Oxford University Press, Oxford, UK, pp. 1–41.

Koshy S. and Radhakrishnan, S. (eds.) (2008) *Transnational South Asians: The Making of a Neo-Diaspora*. Oxford University Press, Oxford, UK.

Kosnick, K. (2007) *Migrant Media*. Indiana University Press, Bloomington, IN.

Kraidy, M. M. (2013) Introduction. In: Kraidy, M. M. (ed.) *Communication and*

*Power in the Global Era: Orders and Borders*. Routledge, London, UK, and New York, pp. 1–8.

Krikorian, M. (February 8, 2013) Illegal-Alien Journalist Jose Antonio Vargas Will Testify Next Week before Senate Judiciary. Will Anyone Arrest Him? *Twitter*. https://twitter.com/MarkSKrikorian/status/299992656526839808.

Kumar, A. (2000) *Passport Photos*. University of California Press, Berkeley, CA.

Kun, J. (2004) What Is an MC if He Can't Rap to Banda? Making Music in Nuevo L.A. *American Quarterly* 56(3), 741–58.

Kundnani, A. (2014) *The Muslims Are Coming: Islamophobia, Extremism, and the Domestic War on Terror*. Verso, London, UK, and New York, NY.

Kymlicka, W. and Norman, W. (1994) Return of the Citizen: A Survey of Recent Work on Citizenship Theory. *Ethics* 104(2), 352–81.

Lacey, M. (August 6, 2010) Border Bill Aims at Indian Companies. *New York Times*. http://www.nytimes.com/2010/08/07/us/politics/07border.html.

Lakhous, A. (2006) *Clash of Civilizations Over an Elevator in Piazza Vittorio*. Europa, New York, NY.

Lampa, G. (2004) Imagining the Blogosphere: An Introduction to the Imagined Community of Instant Publishing. In: Gurak, L., Antonijevic, S., Johnson, L., Ratliff, C., and Reyman, J. (eds.) *Into the Blogsphere: Rhetoric, Community and Culture of Weblogs*. http://blog.lib.umn.edu/blogosphere/imagining_the_blogo sphere.html.

Le, V. (July 25, 2013) 20 Calves that Prove Steve King Is Wrong #NoCantaloupeCalvesHere. *America's Voice*. http://americasvoice.org/blog/20-calves-that-prove-steve-king-wrong.

Lee, C. (2010) Magical Dinners. http://www.newyorker.com/magazine/2010/11/22/magical-dinners.

Legum, J. (July 13, 2006) Rep. King Designs Electrified Fence for Southern Border: "We Do This with Livestock All the Time." *Think Progress*. http://think progress.org/politics/2006/07/13/6259/king-fence.

Lénárt-Cheng, H. and Walker, D. (2011) Recent Trends in Using Life Stories for Social and Political Activism. *Biography* 34(1), 141–79.

Lenhart, A. and Fox, S. (2006) Bloggers: A Portrait of the Internet's New Storytellers. *Pew Internet & American Life Project*. http://www.pewinternet.org/files/old-media/Files/Reports/2006/PIP%20Bloggers%20Report%20July%2019%202006.pdf.pdf.

Leonard, K. (1997) *The South Asian Americans*. Greenwood, Westport, CT.

Leurs, K. (2014) The Politics of Transnational Affective Capital: Digital Connectivity among Young Somalis Stranded in Ethiopia. *Crossings: Journal of Migration and Culture* 5(1), 87–104.

Lindholm, C. (2007) *Culture and Authenticity*. Blackwell, Malden, MA.

Livingstone, S. (2009) On the Mediation of Everything: ICA Presidential Address 2008. *Journal of Communication* 59(1), 1–18.

Löbbermann, D. (2003) Productions of Ethnic Space: Tourism's Narrations. In: Lenz, G. H. and Riese, U. (eds.) *Postmodern New York City: Transfiguring*

*Spaces/Raum-Transformationen.* Heidelberg, Universitätsverlag Winter, pp. 111–36.

Lopez, T. (May 5, 2013) Will the Inclusion of LGBT Couples Threaten the Immigration Bill? *MSNBC.* http://www.msnbc.com/weekends-alex-witt/will-the-inclusion-lgbt-couples-threaten-t.

Lovink, G. (2007) *Zero Comments: Blogging and Critical Internet Culture.* Routledge, New York, NY.

Löwenheim, O. and Gazit, O. (2009) Power and Examination: A Critique of Citizenship Tests. *Security Dialogue* 40(2), 145–67.

Lowney, C. (2009) Authenticity and the Reconciliation of Modernity. Pluralist 4(1), 33–50.

Luibhéid, E. (2002) *Entry Denied: Controlling Sexuality at the Border.* University of Minnesota Press, Minneapolis, MN.

Macdonald, M. (2006) Muslim Women and the Veil: Problems of Image and Voice in Media Representations. *Feminist Media Studies* 6(1), 7–23.

Madianou, M. and Miller, D. (2012) *Migration and New Media: Transnational Families and Polymedia.* Routledge, London, UK.

Maira, S. (2009) *Missing: Youth, Citizenship, and Empire after 9/11.* Duke University Press, Durham, NC.

Malinowski, E. (April 19, 2013) FYI: A Facebook Group Dedicated to Finding Missing Brown Student Was Deleted This Evening. *Twitter.* https://twitter.com/erikmal/status/325141723112144896.

Mallapragada, M. (2006) Home, Homeland, Homepage: Belonging and the Indian-American Web. *New Media & Society* 8(2), 207–27.

Mamdani, M. (2005) *Good Muslim, Bad Muslim: America, the Cold War, and the Roots of Terror.* Harmony, New York, NY.

Mandel, R. (2008) *Cosmopolitan Anxieties: Turkish Challenges to Citizenship and Belonging in Germany.* Duke University Press, Durham, NC.

Mani, B. and Varadarajan, L. (2005) The Largest Gathering of the Global Indian Family: Neoliberalism, Nationalism, and Diaspora at Pravasi Bharatiya Divas. *Diaspora: A Journal of Transnational Studies* 14(1), 45–74.

Mannur, A. (2005) Model Minorities Can Cook: Fusion Cuisine in Asian America. In: Davé, S., Nishime, L., and Oren, T. (eds.) *East Main Street: Asian American Popular Culture.* NYU Press, New York, NY, pp. 72–94.

Mannur, A. (2013) Eat, Dwell, Orient: Food Networks and Asian/American Cooking Communities. *Cultural Studies* 27(4), 585–610.

Manuel, J., Pineda, C., Galisky, A., and Shine, R. (eds.) (2012) *Papers: Stories by Undocumented Youth.* Graham Street Productions, Portland, OR.

Marciniak, K. and Tyler, I. (2014) *Immigrant Protest: Politics, Aesthetics and Everyday Dissent.* State University of New York Press, New York, NY.

Margolis, M. (1993) *Little Brazil.* Princeton University Press, Princeton, NJ.

Martinez, M., Yan, H., and Shoichet, C. E. (July 16, 2014) Growing Protests Over Immigrant Children Hits Arizona. *CNN.* http://www.cnn.com/2014/07/15/us/arizona-immigrant-children.

Mayer, U. (2012) Violent Criminals and Noble Savages. In: Straub, J. (ed.) *Paradoxes of Authenticity: Studies on a Critical Concept.* Transaction, Piscatway, NJ, pp. 185–200.

Mazzarella, W. (2004) Culture, Globalization, Mediation. *Annual Review of Anthropology* 33(1), 345–67.

McKeown, A. M. (2011) *Melancholy Order: Asian Migration and the Globalization of Borders.* Columbia University Press, New York, NY.

McKinnon, S. L. (2009) Citizenship and the Performance of Credibility: Audiencing Gender-Based Asylum Seekers in U.S. Immigration Courts. *Text and Performance Quarterly* 29(3), 205–21.

McNevin, A. (2006) Political Belonging in a Neoliberal Era: The Struggle of the Sans-Papiers. *Citizenship Studies* 10(2), 135–51.

McNevin, A. (2007) Irregular Migrants, Neoliberal Geographies and Spatial Frontiers of "The Political." *Review of International Studies* 33(4), 655–74.

Melwani, L. (July 5, 2014) Bharatnatyam in Jeans. *Little India.* http://www.littlein dia.com/arts-entertainment/1533–bharatnatyam-in-jeans.html.

Mesa, A. (2002) Remembering Victims of Hate Crimes. *Southern Poverty Law Center.* http://www.splcenter.org/get-informed/intelligence-report/browse-all-issues/2002/spring/the-forgotten?page=0,6.

Mitchell, T. (2000) Introduction. In: Mitchell, T. (ed.) *Questions of Modernity.* University of Minnesota Press, Minneapolis, MN, pp. xi–xxvii.

Mitchell, W. J. T. and Hansen, M. B. N. (2010) *Critical Terms for Media Studies.* University of Chicago Press, Chicago, IL.

Mitra, A. (2001) Marginal Voices in Cyberspace. *New Media and Society* 3, 29–48.

Mitra, A. (2008) Using Blogs to Create Cybernetic Space Examples from People of Indian Origin. *Convergence: The International Journal of Research into New Media Technologies* 14(4), 457–72.

Mitropoulos, A. and Neilson, B. (January 8, 2006) Exceptional Times, Non-Governmental Spacings, and Impolitical Movements. *Vacarme.* http://www.vacarme.org/article484.html.

Moallem, M. (2005) *Between Warrior Brother and Veiled Sister: Islamic Fundamentalism and the Politics of Patriarchy in Iran.* University of California Press, Berkeley, CA.

Moorti, S. (2007) Imaginary Homes, Transplanted Traditions: The Transnational Optic and the Production of Tradition in Indian Television. *Journal of Creative Communications* 2(1–2), 1–21.

Morley, D. (2000) *Home Territories: Media, Mobility and Identity.* Routledge, London, UK.

Morley, D. (2011) Communications and Transport: The Mobility of Information, People and Commodities. *Media, Culture & Society* 33(5), 743–59.

Morrissey, M. (2013) A DREAM Disrupted: Undocumented Migrant Youth Disidentifications with U.S. Citizenship. *Journal of International and Intercultural Communication* 6(2), 145–62.

Mulholland, R. (June 29, 2014a) Marine Le Pen Calls for End to Dual Nationality after Algeria's World Cup Celebrations Turn Violent. *Telegraph*. http://www.telegraph.co.uk/news/worldnews/europe/france/10933990/Marine-Le-Pen-calls-for-end-to-dual-nationality-after-Algerias-World-Cup-celebrations-turn-violent.html.

Mulholland, R. (June 30, 2014b) Nice Mayor Bans Foreign Flags Ahead of World Cup Riot Fears. *Telegraph*. http://www.telegraph.co.uk/news/worldnews/europe/france/10935738/Nice-mayor-bans-foreign-flags-ahead-of-World-Cup-riot-fears.html.

Naficy, H. (2007) Foreword: On the Global Inter-, Multi- and Trans-. In: Grossman, A. and O'Brien, Á. (eds.) *Projecting Migration: Transcultural Documentary Practice*. Wallflower Press, London, UK, pp. xiii–v.

Nair, P. (2012) The Body Politic of Dissent: The Paperless and the Indignant. *Citizenship Studies* 16(5–6), 783–92.

Najmabadi, A. (2006) Gender and Secularism of Modernity: How Can a Muslim Woman Be French? *Feminist Studies* 32(2), 239–55.

Nakamura, L. (2009) The Socioalgorithmics of Race: Sorting It Out in Jihad Worlds. In: Magnet, S. and Gates, K. (eds.) *The New Media of Surveillance*. Routledge, New York, NY, 149–61.

Narayan, S. (December 30, 2010) In Their Own Voice – Shedding the NRI Tag. *Hindu*. http://www.thehindu.com/arts/music/article1018586.ece.

Narayan, U. (1997) *Dislocating Cultures: Identities, Traditions, and Third World Feminism*. Routledge, New York, NY.

Ngai, M. M. (2003) *Impossible Subjects: Illegal Aliens and the Making of Modern America*. Princeton University Press, Princeton, NJ.

Nir, S. M., Cohen, P., and Rashbaum, W. K. (August 16, 2013) Struggling Immigrant Artist Tied to $80 Million New York Fraud. *New York Times*. http://www.nytimes.com/2013/08/17/nyregion/struggling-immigrant-artist-tied-to-80-million-new-york-fraud.html.

Nyers, P. (2003) Abject Cosmopolitanism: The Politics of Protection in the Anti-Deportation Movement. *Third World Quarterly* 24(6), 1069–93.

Nyers, P. (2008) No One Is Illegal Between City and Nation. In: Isin, E. F. and Nielsen, G. M. (eds.) *Acts of Citizenship*. Zed Books, New York, NY, pp. 160–81.

Nyers, P. (2010) No One Is Illegal Between City and Nation. *Studies in Social Justice* 4(2), 127–43.

O'Brien, S. A. (February 24, 2015) Immigrant Spouses Find Relief with New H-4 Visa Rule. *CNN Money*. http://money.cnn.com/2015/02/24/news/economy/h4-visa-immigration.

Oliveri, F. (2012) Migrants as Activist Citizens in Italy: Understanding the New Cycle of Struggles. *Citizenship Studies* 16(5–6), 793–806.

Ong, A. (1999) *Flexible Citizenship*. Duke University Press, Durham, NC.

Ong, A. (2006) *Neoliberalism as Exception: Mutations in Citizenship and Sovereignty*. Duke University Press, Durham, NC.

Orgad, S. (2012) *Media Representation and the Global Imagination*. Polity, Cambridge, UK.

Ossman, S. (2007) Linked Comparisons for Life and Research. In: Ossman, S. (ed.) *The Places We Share: Migration, Subjectivity, and Global Mobility*. Lexington, New York, NY, pp. 201–18.

Padios, J. M. (2011) Dial "C" for Culture: Telecommunications, Gender and the Filipino Transnational Migrant Market. In: Hegde, R. S. (ed.) *Circuits of Visibility: Gender and Transnational Media Cultures*. NYU Press, New York, NY, pp. 212–30.

Pain, R. and Smith, S. (2008) Fear: Geopolitics and Everyday Life. In: Pain, R. and Smith, S. (eds.) *Fear: Critical Geopolitics and Everyday Life*. Routledge, New York, NY, pp. 1–23.

Panagakos, A. N. and Horst, H. A. (2006) Return to Cyberia: Technology and the Social Worlds of Transnational Migrants. *Global Networks* 6(2), 109–24.

Papacharissi, Z. A. (2010) *A Private Sphere: Democracy in a Digital Age*. Polity, Cambridge, UK.

Papadopoulos, D. and Tsianos, V. (2013) After Citizenship: Autonomy of Migration, Organizational Ontology and Mobile Commons. *Citizenship Studies* 17(2), 178–96.

Papadopoulos, D., Stephenson, N., and Tsianos, V. (2008) *Escape Routes: Control and Subversion in the 21st Century*. Pluto Press, London, UK.

Papastergiadis, N. (2000) *The Turbulence of Migration*. Polity, Cambridge.

Papastergiadis, N. (2009) Wog Zombie: The De- and Re-Humanisation of Migrants, from Mad Dogs to Cyborgs. *Cultural Studies Review* 15(2), 147–78.

Parker, A. (March 18, 2013) Gender Bias Seen in Visas for Skilled Workers. *New York Times*. http://www.nytimes.com/2013/03/19/us/politics/gender-bias-seen-in-visas-for-skilled-workers.html.

Payne, R. (2013) Virality 2.0: Networked Promiscuity and the Sharing Subject. *Cultural Studies* 27(4), 540–60.

Penketh, A. and Borger, J. (January 7, 2015) Fight Intimidation with Controversy: Charlie Hebdo's Response to Critics. *Guardian*. http://www.theguardian.com/world/2015/jan/07/charlie-hebdo-satire-intimidation-analysis.

Ponzanesi, S. and Leurs, K. (2014) On Digital Crossings in Europe. In: Ponzanesi, S. and Leurs, K. (eds.) Special issue on Digital Crossings in Europe. *Crossings: Journal of Migration and Culture* 4(1), pp. 3–22.

Prashad, V. (2000) *The Karma of Brown Folk*. University of Minnesota Press, Minneapolis, MN.

Preston, J. (August 13, 2010) Obama Signs Border Bill to Increase Surveillance. *New York Times*. http://www.nytimes.com/2010/08/14/us/politics/14immig.html.

Puar, J. K., and Rai, A. (2002) Monster, Terrorist, Fag: The War on Terrorism and the Production of Docile Patriots. *Social Text* 20(3), 117–48.

Pugliese, J. (2006) Asymmetries of Terror: Visual Regimes of Racial Profiling and the Shooting of Jean Charles de Menezes in the Context of the War in Iraq.

*Borderlands e-journal* 5(1). http://www.borderlands.net.au/vol5no1_2006/pug-liese.htm.

Punathambekar, A. (2005) Bollywood in the Indian-American Diaspora: Mediating a Transitive Logic of Cultural Citizenship. *International Journal of Cultural Studies* 8(2), 151–73.

Purkayastha, B. (2005) *Negotiating Ethnicity: Second Generation South Asian Americans Traverse a Transnational World.* Rutgers University Press, New Brunswick, NJ.

Purkayastha, B. (2009) Another World of Experience? Transnational Contexts and the Experiences of South Asian Americans. *South Asian Diaspora* 1(1), 85–99.

Quayson, A. and Daswani, G. (2013) Introduction. Diaspora and Transnationalism: Scapes, Scales and Scopes. In: Quayson, A. and Daswani, G. (eds.) *A Companion to Diaspora and Transnationalism.* Wiley-Blackwell, Malden, MA, pp. 1–26.

Radhakrishnan, R. (1996) *Diasporic Mediations: Between Home and Location.* University of Minnesota Press, Minneapolis, MN.

Radio France International (July 1, 2014) European Court Upholds French Full Veil Ban. *BBC News.* http://www.bbc.com/news/world-europe-28106900.

Raj, D. (2003) *Where Are You From? Middle Class Migrants in the Modern World.* University of California Press, Berkeley, CA.

Rajagopal, A. (2001) *Politics after Television: Hindu Nationalism and the Reshaping of the Public in India.* Cambridge University Press, Cambridge, UK.

Rajagopal, A. (September 29, 2014) India's Controversial Leader Gets Rock Star Treatment in U.S. *The Takeaway with John Hockenberry.* http://www.thetake away.org/story/india-controversial-leader-gets-rock-star-treatment-in-us.

Ramakrishnan, M. V. (January 29, 2010) Impressive Roll-Call! *Hindu.* http://www.thehindu.com/todays-paper/tp-features/tp-fridayreview/article788976. ece.

Ramos-Zayas, A. Y. (2003) *National Performances: The Politics of Class, Race, and Space in Puerto Rican Chicago.* University of Chicago Press, Chicago, IL.

Rancière, J. (2004) *Disagreement: Politics and Philosophy.* Rose, J. (trans.). University of Minnesota Press, Minneapolis, MN.

Rancière, J. and Lie, T. (August 11, 2006) Our Police Order: What Can Be Said, Seen, and Done. *Eurozine.* http://www.eurozine.com/articles/ 2006-08-11-lieranciere-en.html.

Rancière, J. and Panagia, D. (2000) Dissenting Words: A Conversation with Jacques Rancière. *Diacritics* 30(2), 113–26.

Ravindran, S. (March 1, 2010) Ether Music: Online Classical Lessons Have Restored the Guru-Shishya Harmony Across Continents. *Outlook.* http://www. outlookindia.com/article.aspx?264326.

Ray, K. (2004) *The Migrant's Table: Meals and Memories in Bengali-American Households.* Temple University Press, Philadelphia, PA.

Ray, K. and Srinivas, T. (2012) Introduction. In: Ray, K. and Srinivas, T. (eds.) *Curried Cultures: Globalization, Food, and South Asia.* University of California Press, Berkeley, CA, pp. 3–28.

Reitman, J. (July 17, 2013) Jahar's World. *Rolling Stone*. http://www.rollingstone. com/culture/news/jahars-world-20130717.

Rettberg, J. W. (2008) *Blogging*. Polity, Cambridge, UK.

Rigby, J. and Schlembach, R. (2013) Impossible Protest: No Borders in Calais. *Citizenship Studies* 17(2), 157–72.

Riley, D. (2000) *The Words of Selves: Identification, Solidarity, Irony*. Stanford University Press, Stanford, CA.

Rouse, R. (1992) Making Sense of Settlement: Class Transformation, Cultural Struggle and Transnationalism Among Mexican Migrants in the United States. *Annals of the New York Academy of Sciences* 645, 25–52.

Roy, P. (2010) *Alimentary Tracts: Appetites, Aversions, and the Postcolonial*. Duke University Press, Durham, NC.

Rubin, R. and Melnick, J. P. (2007) *Immigration and American Popular Culture: An Introduction*. NYU Press, New York, NY.

Russell, A. and Echchaibi, N. (2009) Introduction. In: Russell, A. and Echchaibi, N. (eds.) *International Blogging: Identity, Politics, and Networked Publics*. Peter Lang, New York, NY.

Russert, L. (April 19, 2013) It's Still Early w Unconfirmed Scanner Reports but if Reddit Was Right with the Sunil Tripathi Theory, It's Changed the Game 4ever. *Twitter*. https://twitter.com/LukeRussert/status/325142594571083776.

Said, E. W. (1975) *Beginnings: Intentions and Method*. Columbia University Press, New York, NY.

Said, E. W. (2000) The Clash of Definitions. In: Said, A. *Reflections on Exile and Other Essays*. Harvard University Press, Cambridge, MA, pp. 569–92.

Santhanagopalan, N. (December 26, 2010) In Their Own Voice: e-Guru, Guru, You-Guru. *Hindu*. http://www.thehindu.com/features/friday-review/music/article981424.ece.

Sarlin, B. (2013) DREAMers Deliver Cantaloupes to House Members Who Voted with Steve King. http://www.msnbc.com/hardball/dreamers-deliver-cantaloupes-house-members.

Sassen, S. (1998) *Globalization and Its Discontents*. New Press, New York, NY.

Sassen, S. (1999) *Guests and Aliens*. New Press, New York, NY.

Saxenian, A. (2006) *The New Argonauts: Regional Advantage in a Global Economy*. Harvard University Press, Cambridge, MA.

Sayad, A. (2004) *The Suffering of the Immigrant*. Macey, D. (trans.). Polity, Cambridge, UK.

Schuessler, J. (May 4, 2015) Charlie Hebdo Award at PEN Gala Sparks More Debate. *New York Times*. http://www.nytimes.com/2015/05/05/books/charlie-hebdo-award-at-pen-gala-sparks-more-debate.html?_r=0.

Scott, J. W. (2002) Feminist Reverberations. *differences: A Journal of Feminist Cultural Studies* 13(3), 1–23.

Scott, J. W. (2007) *The Politics of the Veil*. Princeton University Press, Princeton, NJ.

Seitz-Wald, A. (May 22, 2012) Rep. Steve King: Immigrants Are Like Dogs. *Salon*. http://www.salon.com/2012/05/22/rep_steve_king_immigrants_like_dogs.

Selvon, S. (1956) *The Lonely Londoners*. Longman, New York, NY.

Semple, K. (August 1, 2008) A $126 Million Rumor, Flying from New Jersey to Rio. *New York Times*. http://www.nytimes.com/2008/08/01/nyregion/01jack pot.html.

Seremetakis, N. (1994) The Memory of the Senses, Part II: Still Acts. In: Seremetakis, N. (ed.) *The Senses Still*. University of Chicago Press, Chicago, IL, pp. 23–45.

Serfaty, V. (2004) *The Mirror and the Veil: An Overview of American Online Diaries and Blogs*. Rodopi, Amsterdam, Netherlands.

Sharma, N. T. (2010) *Hip Hop Desis: South Asian Americans, Blackness and a Global Race Consciousness*. Duke University Press, Durham, NC.

Shashikiran, K. N. (February 23, 2010) Money Matters in Carnatic Music. http://mycarnatic.org/blogs/?p=199.

Shichor, Y. (2010) Net Nationalism: The Digitalization of the Uyghur Diaspora. In: Alonso, A. and Oiarzabal, P. J. (eds.) *Diasporas in the New Media Age: Identity, Politics and Community*. University of Nevada Press, Las Vegas, NV, pp. 291–316.

Shukla, S. (2003) *India Abroad: Diasporic Cultures of Postwar America and England*. Princeton University Press, Princeton, NJ.

Silverstone, R. (2002) Complicity and Collusion in the Mediation of Everyday Life. *New Literary History* 33(4), 761–80.

Silverstone, R. (2005) The Sociology of Mediation and Communication. In: Calhoun, C., Rojek, C., and Turner, B. (eds.) *The SAGE Handbook of Sociology*. Sage, London, UK, pp. 188–207.

Soysal, Y. (1995) *Limits of Citizenship: Migrants and Postnational Membership in Europe*. University of Chicago Press, Chicago, IL.

Spivak, G. (1999) *A Critique of Postcolonial Reason: Toward a History of the Vanishing Present*. Harvard University Press, Cambridge, MA.

Squire, V. (2011) The Contested Politics of Mobility: Politicizing Mobility, Mobilizing Politics. In: Squire, V. (ed.) *The Contested Politics of Mobility: Borderzones and Irregularity*. Routledge, New York, NY, pp. 1–26.

Sreberny, A. and Khiabany, G. (2010) *Blogistan: The Internet and Politics in Iran*. Taurus, London, UK.

Standing, G. (2011) *The Precariat: The New Dangerous Class*. Bloomsbury, London, UK, and State University of New York Press, Albany, NY.

Stanmeyer, J. (2014) https://www.worldpressphoto.org/content/american-photographer-john-stanmeyer-wins-world-press-photo-year-2013.

Straw, J. (October 6, 2006) I Want to Unveil My Views on an Important Issue. *Telegraph*. http://www.telegraph.co.uk/news/1530718/I-want-to-unveil-my-views-on-an-important-issue.html.

Sturcke, J. (October 2, 2008) Sir Ian Blair Profile: Commissioner of Controversy. *Guardian*. http://www.theguardian.com/politics/2008/aug/20/ian.blair.profile.

Subramanian, L. (2008) *New Mansions for Music: Performance, Pedagogy and Criticism.* Social Science Press, New Delhi, India.

Subramaniam, S. (December 1, 2006) The Future of Carnatic Music Is in the U.S. http://archives.chennaionline.com/music/Carnaticmusic/2006/11us-carnatic. asp.

Subramanian, S. (December 12, 2008) Carnatic Music Now in New Media Formats. *Live Mint.* http://www.livemint.com/2008/12/12234510/Carnatic-music-now-in-new-medi.html.

Suebsaeng, A. (April 19, 2013) My Innocent Brother Was Made Into a Bombing Suspect: Sunil Tripathi's Sister Speaks. *Mother Jones.* http://www.motherjones. com/mojo/2013/04/sunil-tripathi-sister-sangeeta-media-labelling-her-brother-bombing-suspect.

Sugarman, J. C. (2004) Diasporic Dialogues: Mediated Musics and the Albanian Transnation. In: Turino, T. and Lea, J. (eds.) *Identity and the Arts in Diaspora Communities.* Harmonie Park Press, Warren, MI, pp. 21–38.

Suhasini, L. (June 6, 2010) Global Tutorials. *Mid Day.* http://www.mid-day.com/ articles/global-tutorials/84398.

Sun, F. (June 14, 2012) Behind the Cover: America's Undocumented Immigrants. *Time.* http://lightbox.time.com/2012/06/14/behind-the-cover-americas-undoc umented-immigrants/#2.

Tagg, J. (1993) *Burden of Representation: Essays on Photographies and Histories.* University of Minnesota, Minneapolis, MN.

Tarlo, E. (2010) *Visibly Muslim: Fashion, Politics, Faith.* Bloomsbury, London, UK.

Terranova, T. (2000) Free Labor: Producing Culture for the Digital Economy. *Social Text* 18(2), 33–58.

Thacker, E. (2005) *The Global Genome: Biotechnology, Politics, and Culture.* MIT Press, Cambridge, MA.

This American Life from WBEZ (March 3, 2014) 520: No Place Like Home. *Chicago Public Radio.* http://www.thisamericanlife.org/radio-archives/episode/ 520/no-place-like-home.

*Time* (July 8, 1985) Immigrants: The Changing Face of America. Special issue. *Time.*

*Time* (November 18, 1993) The New Face of America: How Immigrants Are Shaping the World's First Multicultural Society. Special issue. *Time.*

*Time* (June 25, 2012) We Are Americans: Just Not Legally. *Time.*

Thompson, J. B. (1995) *The Media and Modernity: A Social Theory of the Media.* Stanford University Press, Stanford, CA.

Tomlinson, C. (April 19, 2013) The US Must Guard Against a Jean Charles de Menezes Disaster after Boston. *Huff Post.* http://www.huffingtonpost.co.uk/ claudia-tomlinson/boston-jean-charles-de-menezes_b_3113071.html.

Trilling, L. (1972) *Sincerity and Authenticity.* Harvard University Press, Cambridge, MA.

Tsagarousianou, R. (2004) Rethinking the Concept of Diaspora: Mobility,

Connectivity and Communication in a Globalized World. *Westminster Papers in Communication and Culture* 1(1), 52–66.

Tyler, I. and Marciniak, K. (2013) Immigrant Protest: An Introduction. *Citizenship Studies* 17(2), 143–56.

Uma Devi, S. (2002) Globalisation, Information Technology and Asian Indian Women in US. *Economic and Political Weekly* 37(43), 4421–8.

Valdivia, A. (2010) *Latino/as in the Media*. Polity, Cambridge, UK.

Van der Veer, P. (1995) Introduction. In: Van der Veer, P. (ed.) *Nation and Migration: The Politics of Space in the South Asian Diaspora*. University of Pennsylvania Press, Philadelphia, PA, pp. 1–16.

Van der Veer, P. (2005) Virtual India: Indian IT Labor and the Nation-State. In: Hansen, T. B. and Stepputat, F. (eds.) *Sovereign Bodies: Citizens, Migrants, and States in the Postcolonial World*. Princeton University Press, Princeton, NJ, pp. 276–90.

Van Dijck, J. (2007) *Mediated Memories in the Digital Age*. Stanford University Press, Stanford, CA.

Van Dijck, J. (2013) *The Culture of Connectivity: A Critical History of Social Media*. Oxford University Press, Oxford, UK.

Van Doorn, N. (2011) Digital Spaces, Material Traces: How Matter Comes to Matter in Online Performances of Gender, Sexuality and Embodiment. *Media, Culture & Society* 33(4), 531–47.

Vargas, J. A. (June 22, 2011) My Life as an Undocumented Immigrant. *New York Times*. http://www.nytimes.com/2011/06/26/magazine/my-life-as-an-undocumented-immigrant.html?pagewanted=all&_r=1&.

Vargas, J. A. (2012a) Immigration Debate: The Problem with the Word *Illegal*. *Time*. http://ideas.time.com/2012/09/21/immigration-debate-the-problem-with-the-word-illegal.

Vargas, J. A. (2012b) Not Legal, Not Leaving. *Time*. http://content.time.com/time/magazine/article/0,9171,2117243,00.html.

Vargas, J. A. (September 20, 2012c) Keynote Address. *Online News Association Conference*. http://ona12.journalists.org/sessions/friday-morning-keynote-jose-antonio-vargas.

Vargas, J. A. (January 31, 2013a) Vargas Hosts White House Immigration Hangout. Interview with Jacob Sobaroff. *Huffpost live*. http://live.huffingtonpost.com/r/segment/jose-antonio-vargas-white-house/510ae37002a760339b000446.

Vargas, J. A. (February 8, 2013b) @MarkSKrikorian, I look Forward to Seeing You There, Mark. If You Want to Get Me Arrested, Go Ahead. Nothing to Fear but Fear Itself. *Twitter*. https://twitter.com/MarkSKrikorian/status/299992656526839808.

Vargas, J. A. (February 13, 2013c) Testimony to Senate Judiciary Committee. http://www.judiciary.senate.gov/imo/media/doc/2-13-13VargasTestimony.pdf.

Vasta, E. (2010) Immigrants and the Paper Market: Borrowing, Renting and Buying Identities. *Ethnic and Racial Studies* 34(2), 187–206.

Vaughan-Williams, N. (2007) The Shooting of Jean Charles de Menezes: New Border Politics? *Alternatives: Global, Local, Political* 32(2), 177–95.

Vertovec, S. (2004) Cheap Calls: The Social Glue of Migrant Transnationalism. *Global Networks* 4(2), 219–24.

Vertovec, S. (2009) *Transnationalism.* Routledge, New York, NY.

Ware, V. (2006) Info-War and the Politics of Feminist Curiosity: Exploring New Frameworks for Feminist Intercultural Studies. *Cultural Studies* 20(6), 526–51.

Warner, M. (2002) *Publics and Counterpublics.* Zone Books, New York, NY, and Cambridge, MA.

Weidman, A. (2006) *Singing the Classical, Voicing the Modern: The Postcolonial Politics of Music in South India.* Duke University Press, Durham, NC.

Weiss, A. S. (2011) Authenticity. *Gastronomica: The Journal of Food and Culture* 11(4), 74–7.

Williams, P. J. (November 9, 2006) Keeping Up Appearances. *Nation.* http://www.thenation.com/article/keeping-appearances.

Willig, R. (2012) Recognition and Critique: An Interview with Judith Butler. *Distinktion: Scandinavian Journal of Social Theory* 13(1), 139–44.

Wilstein, W. (July 23, 2013) Rep. Steve King: Immigrants Mostly "Evil" Marijuana-Smugglers with "Calves the Size of Cantaloupes." *Mediaite.* http://www.mediaite.com/tv/rep-steve-king-immigrants-mostly-evil-marijuana-smugglers-with-calves-the-size-of-cantaloupes.

Wimmer, A. and Glick Schiller, N. (2002) Methodological Nationalism and Beyond: Nation-State Building, Migration and the Social Sciences. *Global Network* 2(4), 301–34.

Witteborn, S. (2014) Forced Migrants, Emotive Practice and Digital Heterotopia. *Crossings: Journal of Migration and Culture* 5(1), 73–85.

Yuhas, A. (April 29, 2015). Two Dozen Writers Join Charlie Hebdo PEN Award Protest. *Guardian.* http://www.theguardian.com/books/2015/apr/29/writers-join-protest-charlie-hebdo-pen-award.

Zlotnick, S. (1996) Domesticating Imperialism: Curry and Cookbooks in Victorian England. *Frontiers: A Journal of Women Studies* 16(2/3), 51–68.

Zolberg, A. R. (2006) *A Nation by Design.* Harvard University Press, Cambridge, MA.

Zylinska, J. (2005) *The Ethics of Cultural Studies.* Continuum, London, UK.

# Index

border controls (*cont.*)
  and undocumented immigrants 23–4,
    25, 26, 27–8
Boston Marathon bombing 19, 41–8, 50
boyd, d. 69
Brah, A. 17
*Brazilian Voice* 1
Buettner, E. 75
Bunting, M. 64
bureaucracy, power of 107
Bush, George W.
  and terrorism 43
Bush, Laura 62
Butler, J. 22, 23, 27, 40, 48
Buzz Feed
  and the Boston Marathon bombing 44

Cacho, L. M. 111
call centers
  deportees and employment in 118
Canada
  Indian diaspora in 73, 79, 117
capitalism
  capital flows and diasporic communities
    7
  communicative capitalism and diasporic
    food blogs 84
  *see also* global capital
Carey, Peter 120
Caribbean immigrants in Britain
  in Selvon's *The Lonely Londoners* 13–14
Carnatic music 2, 20, 93–105
  and authenticity 99, 102–5
  education in 96–7, 97–8, 100–2
  and identity as cultural literacy 95–7
  and immigrant communities 96
  maintaining cultural and aesthetic
    fidelity 94–5
  South Asian musicians 93–4, 98, 101–4
Chakrabarty, D. 65
*Charlie Hebdo* 120–1
Chavez, Leo 112
children
  undocumented immigrants 16–17
Chinese immigrants
  Qian and art forgery 88–9
  and the US Page Law (1875) 108
Chow, R. 51
cities *see* global cities; New York City
citizenship
  and anti-immigrant protest groups
    16–17
  and authenticity 86–8

citizens and recognition of immigrants
    39–41
  debates on the meaning of 2
  and diasporic communities 7, 8, 11
  and document power 107
  dual 107
  naturalized citizens 8, 106
  and the neoliberal economy 117, 119
  official narratives of 4
  tests 109
  thick and thin versions of 25, 31
  and undocumented immigrants 18, 21,
    22–3, 24–7, 31, 36, 38
  and veiled Muslim women 53, 54, 58,
    59, 63–4, 66–7
*Clash of Civilizations Over an Elevator in
  Piazza Vittorio* (Lakhous) 86
class
  and migration narratives 13–14
  *see also* middle-class diaspora (in the US)
Clifford, James 105
Cole, Teju 120
Coleman, E. G. 71
colonialism
  and Algerian immigrants in France 87
  and diasporic food blogs 79
  and veiled Muslim women 62, 66
connectivity
  and diasporic cultures 105
  and diasporic food blogs 69–70, 84
  technologies of 9, 11, 12–13
consumerism
  and authenticity 91, 92
  and the diaspora 17, 20
cookbooks
  and Indian diasporic food blogs 74, 78,
    81, 82
cosmopolitanism
  and diasporic communities in global
    cities 114
  and diasporic food blogs 69, 70, 78–9,
    81, 84
  and veiled Muslim women 58, 61
Coudry, N. 15
Coulter, Ann 87
Coutin, S. B. 8
crowd-sourcing
  and the Boston Marathon bombing
    44–5
culinary flexibility
  and diasporic food blogs 79–81
cultural citizenship
  and the neoliberal economy 119